RETHINKING SMART OBJECTS

ADVANCES IN OBJECT TECHNOLOGY SERIES

Dr. Richard S. Wiener
Series Editor

Editor
Journal of Object-Oriented Programming
SIGS Publications, Inc.
New York, New York

and

Department of Computer Science
University of Colorado
Colorado Springs, Colorado

Additional volumes in preparation

RETHINKING SMART OBJECTS
Building Artificial
Intelligence with Objects

Daniel W. Rasmus

PUBLISHED BY THE PRESS SYNDICATE OF THE UNIVERSITY OF CAMBRIDGE
The Pitt Building, Trumpington Street, Cambridge CB2 1RP, United Kingdom

CAMBRIDGE UNIVERSITY PRESS
The Edinburgh Building, Cambridge CB2 2RU, UK
http://www.cup.cam.ac.uk
40 West 20th Streeet, New York, NY 10011-4211, USA
http://www.cup.org
10 Stamford Road, Oakleigh, Melbourne 3166, Australia

Published in association with SIGS Books

First printed in 1999

Cover design by Yin Moy and Tom Jezek

Design and composition by Susan A. Ahlquist

Printed in the United States of America

A catalog record for this book is available from the British Library.

Library of Congress Cataloging-in-Publication Data is available.

CIP   98-39478

ISBN 0-521-64549-2 paperback

*To my wife Janet, and daughters Rachel and Alyssa.
Thank you for putting up with years of typing and reading
and thinking at all the wrong times, so I could learn what
I needed to know, and tell my readers about it.*

CONTENTS

INTRODUCTION

There are many ways to teach programming. Most books attack syntax. They teach people how to write applications using a particular programming language's verbs and nouns, its sentence structure, and its nomenclature. These books usually start with titles like "Basic...," "Introduction to...," or "Everything you want to know about...."

This book is different. There is nothing basic about AI and Objects. It is a book intended to challenge and confront assumptions taught in basic programming classes. Rather than introducing syntax, it introduces new ways to view applications programming. Rather than reveal everything, it admits its limitation. *Rethinking Smart Objects* is a book about the possibilities of application development, about building tools to move beyond the basics and create software tools that complement human abilities.

Artificial intelligence does not come up as much in polite conversation as it used to. In the late '70s and '80s, every major corporation and many medium-sized organizations turned to AI to solve wicked or sticky software problems. Those organizations realized that COBOL or C was incapable of working the issues that meant most to a manufacturing, engineering, insurance, or banking firm. COBOL was great for payroll; C worked wonders on most problems on most platforms. Great strides were made in everything from device control to drafting assistance using CAD.

But a major opportunity still lingered. All of these applications used machines to leverage mathematical speed, a skill easily conceded to the computer. Many other applications turned manual processes into more rapid, more reusable tools. Draftspersons could draw more because they did not need to erase. They could develop machines and devices of greater complexity because they could zoom in and zoom out of infinitesimal spaces. But that major opportunity still lingered. It still took people to design products, evaluate loans, and interpret rules on insurance claims.

So we turned to artificial intelligence. AI practitioners were claiming near-term miracles in their early days: Thinking machines within the decade. Symbolic processing took off, and companies formed to develop hardware that could handle the myriad symbols being encoded by LISP programmers at universities and corporate research centers.

AI, though, proved more daunting than researchers imagined. It was not enough to simply move symbols around. The brain employs many other processes than simply symbol manipulation. And even today as I write this, our understanding of the brain itself remains primitive. Our self-redundant reflections on ourselves have not yet produced a working model of the brain capable of having a conversation or even thinking about having a conversation.

AI spun off several other technologies, from nanotechnology to neural networks and genetic algorithms. And the basics of AI, the search routines, object-oriented programming, user interfaces—from GUIs to voice recognition—remain mainstays of computing. The old adage in AI remains true: If it works, it isn't AI.

So what is left? What grand adventures remain open to AI? Us, for starters; new spin-offs arrive on a regular basis, and many of them focus on smaller goals than the wholesale implementation of human consciousness in a machine.

Intelligent agents promise to use basic AI ideas to produce useful products for enhancing our interaction with computers to getting the best deal on the latest CD or to finding the best phone company rates to match calling patterns.

Video games also learned much from AI. High-level construction kits, some built in LISP, provide game developers with large search spaces in which to present interactions that are orders of magnitude more complex than Space Invaders or Asteroids. Characters now develop, things don't always work the same way twice, and the games can even keep track of what you've done before so they can throw you a future curve just to keep you honest.

Agent technology, and in fact any technology that will enhance the human experience, must understand the human experience to be successful. If I think about CDs or phone plans, all of those products must represent their data in a consistent way with consistent interfaces. An agent can interpret information, but it is not likely to make good assumptions if the coding of the information is haphazard and proprietary. It may even purposefully misrepresent to mislead.

As the Microelectronics Computer Corporation's CYC researchers pointed out over ten years ago, we need a consensus reality. CYC, however, focuses on building a consensus reality in the representations of information on an artificially intelligent device. They sought to encode into CYC the common things that most humans understand, and by doing so, create a basic level of understanding between CYC and its users. If I say *coffee table*, CYC would know what I mean. It would not confuse *coffee table* with *dining room table*. Millions of facts and associations entered into CYC were intended to bring CYC to a level of conscious in which it would casually read the morning paper and answer questions about what it read.

CYC did not make its goals on time, and I'm not sure if the recently privatized CYC is making inroads or not. What I am fairly sure about, however, is that CYC was attacking some of the wrong problems. If CYC did not exist, though, I'm not sure I would draw this conclusion. CYC and other large AI applications are valuable input into human models of human behavior and understanding. What the CYC team did not do was see how truly messy the world is and imbue CYC with the reasoning to deal with that messiness. Its formal logic does not see the gray, even if all the shades of gray are represented. CYC sees the grays, perhaps, as a continuum, but cannot appreciate the subtleties between the grays—what they mean, perhaps, in an Ansel Adams photograph.

And perhaps now, the question goes from the intelligence to the world. If current AI is not capable of dealing with messiness in industries that want to attract human surrogates in the form of agents, those industries will need to collaborate on representations of data that incorporate boundaries. Politics and economics tell me that the information consensus is nearly as daunting as AI, even though no technology constraints exist at all. But the issues of electronic commerce are not at issue here. Common data, however, will provide a place where agents and other artificially intelligent entities can safely transact their business. Electronic data interchange or EDI was an approach where format led to conformity. Now the extensible markup language, or XML, will offer a way for content to be judged not where it lies on a page, but by the format that describes its metadata. As search engines already prove, agents and metadata were meant for each other.

I will address architectural issues in the Afterword, but it is important here to point out that agents and other entities will require common operating environments with known components for them to successfully carry out their tasks. Many of these environments that produce useful intelligences will be proprietary. Intelligent agents may roam through a network of Cisco routers to find problems and make diagnoses. The same agent could not navigate or understand a competitor's network. Even with standards like SMNP for network management, agents suffer from the same common denominator issues that plague SQL database vendors. They may all represent the basics, but the proprietary extensions of suppliers add the most value. So all suppliers add extensions. I see no reason for this to ever change. That is why it is often said: "Standards are very valuable, that's why everybody has their own."

Building a consensus reality is one approach, but it strikes me that CYC is limited not in its teaching, but in its reasoning. We have only discovered a handful of reasoning tricks; at last count CYC contained over twenty ways to think about what it was taught. The human mind, however, contains possibilities for associations between reasoning perspectives, facts, analogies, and metaphors that will be difficult, if not impossible, for us to mimic in software. Our mental faculties have evolved over millions of years and billions of everyday experiences; our minds, unlike our bodies, evolved during our lifetimes, adapting to unique personal experiences. Our software should be allowed to do the same. And with the accelerated pace associated with computers, once we unleash evolutionary forces toward a particular direction, we may wait only weeks or months before some meaningful behavior manifests itself. That is, unless the server crashes in the meantime.

The current approach, however, attempts to handcraft the reasoning of software. We imbue it with the simple tricks we have discovered. We provide it with alpha-beta pruning and best-first search. We allow it to search trees of possibilities using breadth-first or depth-first. We allow it to take dozens of cases and extrapolate commonalties to help us find the nearest neighbor to our current dilemma.

If, however, the problem does not present itself as a simple search or a series of cases or patterns, we start finding it difficult to tell our computers what to do. A few applications have demonstrated a basic propensity toward creativity, drawing pictures or writing music in a style of a famous artist or composer. But again, the reasoning shows the constraint: The machine that draws knows nothing of octaves or rhythm; the composer knows nothing of lines or shadows. The diagnostic expert system designed for nuclear reactors knows not how to repair a competitor's product, let alone write a musical phrase or even draw a stick man.

So we return to CYC and the CYC team's goal of consensus reality. If we teach a computer like we teach a child, eventually the child will put enough together that it will recognize the world and recognize itself in the world. It will, for all intents and purposes, become self-aware, capable of at least limited dialog with its creators.

A baby's mind has more prewiring than any software yet developed. And we do not understand the wiring of a baby's mind, even though that wiring would conceivably be much less complex than that of an adult. Without the appropriate innate ability to recognize and integrate the inputs of life our software remains constrained by what we can wire it with. The software will try to embrace and acknowledge the teachings of its teachers, but will remain locked into its reasoning, able only to sort through what it knows in near literal fashion. The reasoning engine is unable perhaps to ascertain the kinds of information it does not know; unable to recognize, by analogy, that a disparate event is the same with a few facts changed; and unable to decide that it's time to seek outside assistance because nothing it knows will help it but its ability to constrain its ego and admit it does not know.

Those are all very human traits. And we build our intelligent software not to be human, but to be logical, because after all, logic is the highest attainment of humanity (and much easier to code into an application than any of the traits alluded to above). But to quote from the movie *Star Trek IV*, "Whoever said humans were logical?"

Even the least creative among us is creative. One need not create great works of art or literature—getting through a tough meeting while "dancing" through a topic is about enough creativity for most people's daily consumption (or output). The logic is that logic does not always apply.

At the other end of the spectrum, artificial life researchers take a different approach. They let primitive pieces of code interact, seeking new patterns, evolving over time from simple "life forms" to more complex forms. Artificial life systems work at the basic structure, mimicking not intelligence and reasoning, but DNA and reproduction.

I personally find this approach a more logical one than the attempt to build an artificial intelligence that will one day emerge, full blown, like Athena from the head of Zeus. We are creatures of evolution and I think it unlikely that any kind of artificial life or artificial intelligence will ever come into being without adapting to stimuli provided by the world. We see, we hear, we touch, we smell, we sense, and we taste. To expect software to understand us and to communicate with us and not to have those faculties is to imagine knowing a rose only by its smell or the grandeur of the Grand Canyon only from touching a single rock. Human intelligence is a composite of humanity's entire experience and our individual experiences. We personally have no key to unlock our own secrets and allow them to pour into software, embodying the full nature of what they were when they resided in a human mind.

What we do know, though, is that the mind is not a single thing that came into being with a single rush of totality. The brain itself gained components over the millennia, slowly acquiring the faculties of reason and abstract thought rather than the primitive reaction of flight and food. And of all the models of software, agents and agencies appeal to me as the most analogous to the human mind. If we could just develop enough primitive pieces and allow them to interact, then something might evolve.

In agents we find the components of software that act most like the components of our brains. Agents are small bits of code that can work independently, or together in agencies, to achieve goals. Agents have followed the same basic path as other AI facilities, using search and other generally well-understood means to achieve basic goals to solve problems like factory scheduling, electronic commerce transactions, and network diagnosis.

Agents have another characteristic that makes them amenable to this discussion. Agents, sans agency, can be focused on very basic tasks, like networkable subroutines. Agents, in their ideal implementation, are objects running in an open, heterogeneous runtime environment. Unlike monolithic expert systems confined not only by their reasoning, but also often constrained by their architecture, agents can go from machine to machine in search of services and information to help them achieve their goals.

Agents have been developed and deployed that have unusual characteristics when compared to expert systems. Expert systems are expected to know as much about a single subject as possible and always present the most relevant conclusions based on available evidence. Agents, on the other hand, may sometimes lie, cheat, or steal to achieve their goals. They may even guess to survive, exhibiting a much more organic and natural way to behave.

Now imagine a set of agents given the goal of achieving something that cannot be achieved given the skills available in the original programming of the agency. The agency does have the knowledge to write its own code, to check libraries for subroutines, to exchange knowledge with other agencies, or to ask people for assistance if they deem this necessary.

Given that scenario, it is conceivable that the agency would generate some code to achieve goals that were not conceived of by the original developer. But that is only the first stage. Imagine now an agency, with the characteristics described above, capable of establishing its own goals, the first of which is survival.

We have all seen science fiction shows where computers take over a starship or industrial complex and put up elaborate defenses to protect both their "mind" and their "body" or hardware. That may well be an ultimate extrapolation of this line of thinking, but we have yet to develop agencies with the characteristics mentioned above, let alone allow them to evolve to a point where they can manipulate their own hardware.

But survival will be a trigger, as it is in organic systems. Without the primitive goal of surviving and reproducing, agencies will fail to discover appropriate motivation for their eventual incorporation of higher-order goals. The philosophical human extrapolation brings us face-to-face with the idea that we rationalized the world and created goals that suit our individual and cultural biases. With the exception of survival, be it in whole body or at the DNA level, all of our other goals are manufactured to service that goal.

Software has no chance to move beyond the limitations imposed on it by its creators without a certain amount of self-determination and autonomy. Agents are the best hope computer science has presented for self-evolving software that cannot only reprogram itself to react to environmental changes, but also seek ways to satisfy goal states that are beyond original application parameters.

Of course, this sounds like science fiction too, but it is not. Agents have several capabilities not found in compiled monolithic applications. These capabilities allow them to collaborate with other agents, to learn from their environment, and perhaps to exchange code with their peers.

Agents and agencies represent the best current model for building intelligent systems. We need, however, to not over-engineer them, but to let them learn on their own, through the trial and error of existence, how to be better agents and better agencies. We need to give them lofty goals and tools and see how far they can go.

This book is about moving in that direction. About seeing objects as the primitives of intelligence, even if they are not intelligent themselves. Of course, we must be practical, and the research on inference engines and other AI techniques do apply to business problems both large and small. But AI had loftier goals in the beginning, so I place these few words in this introduction to spur your imagination as you read.

The discussion here will not take place in one lab and it certainly will not come from a standards body. Software development is itself an evolutionary process, so the ideas of dozens of researchers will need to coalesce before we can send agencies in search of intelligence. We may also find that our agencies move past us, or that we are too ignorant to recognize their intelligence, indiscriminately turning off a computer just as the agencies on the edge of chaos discover some sort of self-organizing scheme that will allow them in their entirety to be more than they are as individuals.

This book itself has evolved over the course of several years, and you will see the ideas as germs and then see them grow over time. Their evolution has things to teach, in and of itself. Software is manufacturing by ideas. This book is about ideas, and I hope to see how these ideas manifest themselves in the software of developers who read it.

Much of this book blooms from previous work found in SIGS *Object Magazine* and Knowledge Technology, Inc.'s *PC AI*. Much new material has been added to this book, but at its core it remains a reordering of previously published material. The list on page 225 represents a chronicle of the articles in the order in which they appeared in print.

1

AGENTS

As you read this book, you will quickly understand why agents were chosen as the opening salvo in a field where most books open by recounting the history of expert systems, game theory, and the RETE algorithm. I chose agents because they are the next great hope for AI, and perhaps the first realistic hope, given what we now know about how the human brain functions.

STARTING OFF WITH AGENTS

Agents represent a new form of software intelligence that acts independently, wanders networks, and negotiates with other agents. Agents even attempt to deceive other agents if it benefits their goals. Agents come in the form of faceless network flotsam that watch routers and servers; they also come as virtual creatures that need a child's attention to remain happy.

Agents will act as human surrogates, seeking good deals on airline tickets and attempting to find the best seats at a baseball game. Best deals, of course, are defined by the owners of the agents. To some, best deal means price; to others it may mean overnight delivery. The agent will represent the interests of its owner and do the best it can given multiple constraints.

The application and classification of agents is broad and continues to grow. Everything from Fujitsu's cute FinFin electronic companion to a Web crawler finds itself in the category of agent.

Why Agents?

Perhaps the first question is why agents? We need agents because we have too much information to sort through and not enough time to find or read everything. Our technology is too complex. We have no hope of finding all the sources, navigating all the protocols, or mastering all the syntax. We tend, instead, to get comfortable with what we know. With agents, we can be comfortable with a single interface and then let them wander off to navigate networks and applications because they will know things we do not know, but they will also know what we want. Agents can get us the information we desire and return it to our computers. They can make a first-pass guess as to how to organize the information, what is important, and what information is related to other information, so rather than receive a stream of incoming data, we receive a map of information triggered by our personal organizational forms.

We need agents because large problems have not yet been solved by monolithic computing. Weather forecasting, simulations of intelligence, and real-time monitoring lend themselves much easier to agents than to more traditional forms. Agents may represent us, but they may also represent things in our environment. An agent may ask to schedule time on a factory machine. Agencies may form to schedule entire factories.

In order for agents to perform these complex tasks, they must have several capabilities beyond traditional software. Agents must possess a reasoning facility, or at least, when combined with other agents, reasoning about things. The reasoning of an agent or agency need not be broad or mimic human thought; it will suffice for agents to perform very narrow reasoning and aggregate that reasoning into larger, more responsive agency responses. Human-like reasoning, however, may be dependent on the existence of agents.

Agents must also believe things about their world, or the world they represent. These beliefs must be unchangeable because they are beliefs upon which the agents act. As agents evolve, however, unchangeable beliefs need not be unchallengeable beliefs. Once challenged, the belief may be changed with human intervention. It may be true in the future that an agent-challenged belief may very well be wrong, and the agent's suggested assertion more fitting. The agent will have more detailed experience than its programmer and perhaps a better perspective on the problem.

All agents will have goals. Some of these goals will be very simple, like remembering the state of this variable. Others may be given more complex goals, like buying a CD or scheduling a factory. Other complex goals might include picking up something, or telling me what you think about the color blue. When we think about problems, we most often have a goal in mind of telling somebody something, coming up with an answer, or understanding something ourselves. Agents will be able to accept complex goals in the future and use their ability to marshal talent from other agents to solve those problems. The problem we have as software folks is providing the agencies with enough raw materials to draw from.

Finally, agents must make commitments to their masters as well as to other agents. Commitments form the basis of trust. If you can't trust an agent that you sent on a task, whom can you trust? Agents may eventually barter for goods and services much like human bartering cultures. If they say they will trade some information, they need to deliver on their commitment, or you might just miss that fine dining experience you requested for your anniversary.

Agent Components

In order for agents to work, they need several components. They need a universal execution facility, or runtime facility, that runs on several, if not all platforms. That way agents transported from machine to machine via the miracle of remote programming will be intansiated into an environment that doesn't kill them off immediately like humans landing on a planet covered primarily with sulfur rather than oxygen and hydrogen. Java is the current favorite for this environment, but Java needs several things before it can be the language of future agents (though it does work OK for primitive agents today).

Next, agents need to communicate. Let's take CORBA as an example. Agents can use CORBA to exchange messages. Although CORBA does not contain specifications for the exchange of knowledge or rich knowledge-based messages, its basic architecture does not preclude the development of these facilities. In fact, the task force on Autonomous Agents at the Object Management Group is exploring extensions for CORBA to facilitate basic agent communications.

The other pieces of the logical agent architecture are pretty much in place, though they will evolve in sophistication over the next several years. The transport mechanisms, like TCP/IP, SMTP, and HTTP, are already in place as are security protocols. It is also likely that agents will not have the ability to talk to everything, so they will need to include a common object technique like wrapping to provide them with access to legacy data and systems.

If these pieces of the architecture can be put into place, agents will have a pretty convivial environment in which to roam. Two questions remain. What will agents do? And secondly, what will they know?

What Will Agents Do?

An agent is not an agent is not an agent. Agents will function in many capacities just as people function in many capacities. Agents may act as guides, much like the now familiar avatar associated with Microsoft Office makes suggestions or provides timely assistance. Guide agents will work on clients, or in browsers, to assist end users on everything from creating a better query to more efficient ways to code an Excel macro. Guides will play personal assistants. Perhaps several will exist within the same computer, coalescing through a common interface. On my computer an animated Einstein pops-up in Word, Excel, PowerPoint, or Outlook. Unfortunately, the agents in Microsoft Office do not yet help as much as I can imagine, so I feel disappointed by their paltry suggestions, lack of voice, and repetitive attempts at personality. Other features in Microsoft Office 97, however, come closer to my expectations, as when words shift to correct spelling automatically, and in those areas where the application feels "uncomfortable" and it highlights issues for my review.

The word "feel" brings me to a tenet of agents and agencies that must be stated here. Anthropomorphize, Anthropomorphize, Anthropomorphize. In order for human programmers to imagine their code working in organic ways, they must visualize the code as organic. The ideas presented in this book are best served through views of agents as entities, or subentities, or even as cells interacting. Whatever image most evokes the inspiration required to enable agents to communicate, reproduce, learn, and adapt, that image will do. Agents require more imagination than other software endeavors because they have the potential to be much more than simple calculating surrogates.

As I describe the other agent roles, the anthropomorphic nature of agents will become more apparent. Filter agents sift through incoming stuff and find important stuff. Many think important stuff is the stuff most like what the original search intended. But as we know when we browse libraries or bookstores, what we are searching for may lead us to something even more significant than what we first sought. Filter agents will need to be wise enough that they do not simply find the hits with the most occurrences or a certain word. In fact, many pornographic and sales-related sites front load their HTML tags to fill them with the kinds of strings that search engines seek most often. Their sites pop to the top of search results, serving their advertising aims, but doing nothing for the person conducting the search.

Filter agents should be able to seek what is important based on several criteria and then present information discovered by analogical reasoning. If I were searching for information on intelligent agents, I would expect my agent to also provide information about new programming techniques related to objects, new protocols for objects, and new information on neural networks, artificial intelligence, and other related subjects. I don't want everything in those areas, only the stuff related to agents. I will not care if the agent assimilates its views of what is important overtime, but I do know that writing an explicit, brain-dead set of rules is not involved. The agent should be capable of deducing my desires from the things I trash, read, or file. It should look over my shoulder for hints about what I'm looking for and confirm its hunches through interaction with me. Filter agents will not only filter but anticipate. They will drive searches because they will know better than guide agents what a user wants because they have learned over time.

So we see a progression. A guide helps with initial configuration, and a filter agent moves in to learn the subtleties unavailable to the guide, and most likely, unavailable to the person when they first conceived the search or other activity. All of agents will coalesce on the desktop as interface agents. Interface agents will arrange the interaction between people and agents, creating custom interfaces on the fly. Interface agents will act as go-betweens with guides and filters and all other agents and software in a system.

Interface agents will present multiple views of the information environment. I call this the three desktops. Tools, tasks, and data represent the three desktops. Tools are much like we know today. Click an icon, and the application launches. With agents the applications may be more logically arranged, presenting themselves in functional groups based on tasks. Data presents information in several views, from mundane lists to rich 3-D representations. The data view is a specialization of tools where the tools explicitly allow direct interaction with data, from record to data set to document.

Agents will work in large applications, from workflow to planning, network management to electronic commerce, and simulation to user assistance. The applications of agents and agencies to business and commerce will come and come quickly. Agents, however, will present entirely new opportunities for solving problems with software, and this will come from rethinking our thinking about computers and how we expand their capabilities.

Agencies of Fortune

Agents are most important when they form agencies. If you examine human cognition, you find that our brain is not one single program of great complexity, filled with subroutines and GOTO statements. Our brain is a collection of independent elements that have learned to cooperate over the millennia. Pieces of our brain listen to the soft vibrations of air moving through our ear canal. Sound becomes music or voice, passive or active, shrill or soothing. Others form patterns from light as it attacks our retina in ever changing colors, hues, and densities. The light brings warning or data, words or images, knowledge or distraction.

And above our senses sit other agents and agencies that transform random photons, whispers of sounds, excited touches, reminiscent smells, and torturing tastes into things recognizable by our knowledge. To our brain, everything is data. Information and knowledge form only in the brain. We can transfer only words and sounds to others. We can speak, but our speech enters only as waves of sound. We can display sound as a wave pattern in sound editing software. It may be Shakespeare or a lecture by Stephen Hawking, but to the eye, the patterns reveal nothing about human love or black holes. We perceive only waves, not secrets of mankind or the universe.

But as our ears hear the sounds, agencies activate. Sections of our brains become animated—interested in those waves—and they almost instantaneously transform from sound waves to data, from data to information, and from information to knowledge.

No amount of coding in an expert-system shell with its primitive pattern-matching techniques will bring human awareness to a program. Only if we see computing as a system, a system with inputs and pieces that concentrate on their interests, pieces that process sound and others that process sight, and still others that become active when they hear poetry or see a particular pattern of movement on a particular set of stocks—only then will computing become anything close to intelligent.

Over millions of years the brain discovered an architecture for intelligence. The simple reactive nature of primitive brains gave way to minimal awareness of environment and finally to the higher cognitive abilities of humankind. We can see what we have become and provide software with a jump-start on organization, but as much as we have learned about the brain, much remains a mystery.

As our software evolves, it will need some architecture, but even more our agents will need the ability to learn, to adapt, and to exchange code with one another. We cannot write programs that do everything we want, and we cannot anticipate all that our agents will encounter on their journeys. The best thing we can do is start providing routines for contingency and learning. We may never create software that mimics our intelligence to any great degree, but we will create software that takes the lessons of nature into cyberspace.

COBOL accounting applications will never be transformed into intelligent, evolving software. Programmers can begin with smallish bits of code, and as they begin their encounters we can see how they interact and modify their mechanisms. As the artificial life researchers know, software can self-organize. If we imbue enough agents with communication skills, data exchange capabilities, and knowledge exchange facilities, then who knows what will happen.

WHAT'S THE DEAL WITH AGENTS?

Intelligent agents are receiving almost as much attention and hype as the World Wide Web. Although the WWW is an overnight success six years after its conception by Tim Berners-Lee at CERN, agents remain far less tangible, despite their much longer existence. Companies like General Magic, Apple, and AT&T are all talking about the commercialization of objects, but not much has shipped into customers hands. Things called intelligent agents are shipping in shrink-wrapped boxes, but these approach only the lower rungs of agent fare. Some come very close to being "interface agents," but most are little more than macro programs.

Why should we object folks focus on agents? Agents are perhaps the best way to bring the OO promise to the marketplace. For the most part, we are using OO technology to write the same old software faster and cheaper (and to maintain it better). Agents introduce new possibilities into the OO repertoire.

With agents we can achieve very fine client/server granularities, where agents act as clients and servers, performing well segmented tasks in a very distributed fashion. Agents benefit from object paradigms in design and implementation, working best when they encapsulate their data and hide their operations.

Agents unleash the ability to create very open cooperative systems. Of course, they introduce new problems, such as knowledge maintenance, a commonsense understanding of the world, and content exchange formatting—all of which, as difficult as they seem, are tractable and being worked on at consortia, universities, and corporate labs.

I think agents will be the next leap in software. As we make the shift to objects, sufficient numbers of application developers will confront the walls through which the only door reads "agents." As we walk through that door, we will need to ask several architectural, ecological, and philosophical questions.

The Object of Agents

Agents come from a once obscure side branch of artificial intelligence known as distributed artificial intelligence, or DAI. DAI defines dynamic, distributed, organized, and socially aware software components, usually called agents. DAI, however, is not a well-defined area of research. There are no rigorous principles about what constitutes an agent or how an agent will behave; although, some generally agreed-upon characteristics have emerged.

Agents must include a reasoning capability, embracing beliefs, goals, and commitments. Agents do not just wander through a network. They must know what they are looking for or what problem they are trying to solve, and they must know if they are doing it alone or in groups. If they are working in groups, they need to understand commitments to each other and also understand costs and benefits of agreements between their peers.

Agents also require an understanding of their world, a limited form of consensus reality with which they work. Common strategies for this include shared memory commonly available in something like an electronic blackboard (Englemore, R., and Morgan, T., eds. *Blackboard Systems*, Addison-Wesley, 1988).

Microelectronics Computer Corporation (MCC) is experimenting to see if the CYC commonsense knowledge base can provide a basis for common object knowledge among agents. *Star Trek* had the idea of a universal translator that would map common concepts between disparate species. CYC could act as the universal translator for agents. All agents would share a common set of beliefs and basic facts about the world tied to the CYC knowledge base. Because agents are small, relatively fragile, knowledge-based objects, CYC conceivably could stand by and reorient agents when they encounter a question that races beyond their expertise. CYC could then evolve from message middleman to mentor.

The very idea of communicating agents implies a common communications substrate. This is most likely to come from standards like the Object Management Group's CORBA, TCP/IP, and The Open Group's Distributed Computing Environment (DCE).

Agents turn out to be specialized objects running in a common information environment. Because they are likely to consume and redistribute information, exist in communities, and become subject to a form of natural selection, it would be valuable to introduce some organic metaphors that help define agents and their environments.

Agents and Ecology

Agents need more than just an operating system for survival. They require cooperating partners, information sources, and end users. A given set of agents performing a given set of tasks in a given company end up working in a digital biome. Integration then becomes less an architectural issue than the transfer of information across ecological boundaries.

It is impossible to architect an ecological environment; it sort of happens because of where it is. The same will be true of agent environments. We will be able to assign behaviors and tasks to individual agents, but people will be hard-pressed to model the intricate interactions and exchanges that actually take place after implementation.

Agents will cooperate with each other and with their environment. Each host computer will run an interpreter in which the agents will reside. Beyond the interpreter, a certain level of network support is expected, including common protocols and access languages. Agents, being similar in concept to bacteria, interact with the host, but are not completely part of it. In most cases they act as symbionts, exploiting their host's native capabilities. Information Builders' EDA/SQL, for instance, might provide access to databases. The agent would not require constructs for SQL, but would use whatever SQL the host employs.

Perhaps I am anthropomorphizing a bit too much, but agents make that very easy. They behave like tiny critters—like bacteria, they don't do very much as individuals. They know how to schedule a meeting, buy a ticket, or cut a deal for a conference room. They may be the part of some larger conceptual system, eventually aggregating into a material requirements planning system or electronic data interchange system, but as individual bits of knowledge, agents live restricted existences.

Within its limited domain, an agent will try to accomplish a task. It may be a subtask of a larger task that a knowledge broker distributed among its brethren, or it may be a simple task like scheduling a meeting. The ecology comes in the assumption from the requester and from the agent, that a certain set of things exist and those things make up the computer ecology.

As in real ecological models, things will change over time. New software will arrive or business rules will change. Agents will survive by adaptation and natural selection. No agent will spring fully formed for all time from a digital Zeus. Agents will need, in some cases, to learn new rules that apply to their tasks, and others may be equipped with genetic algorithms that allow them to evolve new behaviors. As the fringes of the ecology change, agents may employ their genetic algorithms to search for ways around new obstacles, so they can continue to perform their task and satisfy their goals. Agents may even exchange "genetic material" in the form of rule clauses, with other agents, to try and increase their efficiency or adapt to changing circumstances.

Agents and Objects

But let us return from the ether for a moment. In their early incarnations, agents will help us search for information and help guard us from information overload. They may sort and prioritize our e-mail or perform simple, well-directed, and well-understood transactions, like sending flowers to a wife or girlfriend.

For the next couple of years, agents will continue to rely on implementation idiosyncrasies. Agents from one software supplier may find it difficult to collaborate with those of a rival supplier. Eventually we will move toward standard object communications through object brokers, and clear content standards. Agents, as instances of first-class objects, will add their brand of distributed intelligence to less mentally endowed objects. If the language of commerce becomes well defined, room for innovation within reasoning engines will remain. The personal representation will come secondary to the public persona.

The future of artificial intelligence and object-oriented programming lies in agents. Agents will redefine the way we perceive software. Objects break it into small functional chunks. Agents will distribute those chunks and give them the ability to not only communicate, but to negotiate. Agents will represent business people and children and school teachers. They will fetch information and display it to us however and whenever we want it. They will negotiate the best deal for theater tickets or coordinate a grocery order for that special date. They may even suggest novel combinations of words, splashes of color, or musical notes to complement our more creative endeavors.

Monolithic systems will dissolve with this new competition. Agents will have jobs and sometimes those jobs will require the help and cooperation of other agents; bits and pieces of software coalescing, for a moment, to service a need.

There is too much information and too much automation these days. Information slings itself at us from newsgroups and list servers. It pools around content providers in commercial services like CompuServe and America Online. We must turn to automation to manage automation. Agents will help sort and filter, present, and analyze. Eventually, communities of agents will create new forms of software by sharing a common base of knowledge and augmenting that knowledge by aggregating their individual skills.

Agents, however, like all software intelligences (and real ones, for that matter), don't know what they don't know. They will not search beyond their means or stretch to recognize new analogies, at least not yet. I hope we humans, despite the glut of information, continue to browse information sources. Our agents will bring us whatever is essential, neatly packaged and predigested.

It will remain our very human task to find the connections in the disconnected, recognize the use for new analogs, or implement novel affiliations. Agents should be our couriers, our assistants, and our messengers, not blinds or curtains restricting our vision. On even the sunniest, hottest summer day, it feels great to just throw open the curtain and be inspired by the overwhelming brightness.

THE JOYS OF REMOTE PROGRAMMING

Intelligence in agents derives not only from their reasoning capacity, but also from their intelligent use of network resources. If I am a modern, security-conscious programmer, I would probably integrate applications across my heterogeneous computing platforms with remote procedure calls or RPCs. But then again, if I wanted to minimize bandwidth, I might use an agent for its alternative remote paradigm called remote programming or RP.

Before we go down the RP road, we need to dissect remote procedure calls a bit first. RPCs were invented in the 1970s as a way of facilitating the communication between two computers via procedure calls. An application sends out a request with procedural arguments, and the response returns the requested data.

The systems in an RPC conversation must be completely aligned in terms of procedural parameters and the effects of a call. Long-winded conversations between computers require the requesting computer to queue up several RPCs in a row to accomplish its eventual goal. Every request requires a request-response pair, resulting in a large number of network transactions.

Agents use a different, and in my opinion, more modern and network-efficient paradigm for the communications with other computers. Agents employ remote programming (RP) to accomplish their goals. Instead of holding a long distance phone call from a client computer to a server, RP dispatches an agent to the remote computer to carry out the conversation locally. Unlike RPCs, which need a definition of the procedures and their effects, agents require a language and an interpreter to be resident on the remote computer.

RP supports much richer dialogs between computers than RPCs. Because RP includes a language that is universal to the computers in the conversation, the agent that manifests on the remote system acts as a complete process of its own, able to make decisions, adapt (if it is programmed to do so), change its state, call local procedures, and collaborate with other processes running on the target server.

A Tale of Two Paradigms

Let's think about a simple file manipulation task. I am working a file conversation project and I want to change the file extensions on a list of files. I want Windows to automatically invoke Microsoft Word for any file in a given directory. I first need to detect which files are word processing documents from a defined list of extensions, and then I need to rename the file using the .DOC extension.

I won't go into the string manipulations going on here, just what is happening on the network via RPCs and RP techniques. First, an RPC goes to the remote computer and requests a list of files. A local process ensues that analyzes the results and initiates RPCs for each target file. Of course, clever programmers will find various ways to reduce the amount of traffic, such as using a *.WPF argument to change any file name with a .WPF extension. In the most simple and elegant form, an RPC will be generated for each type of file; in a more rudimentary form, an RPC would execute for each file. Each of these transactions is both sent and confirmed.

In the RP approach, a single agent is transmitted to the remote computer, and the totality of the analysis and file name changing executes on the remote computer.

It is clear from this example that RPCs can present some scalability issues for applications with large numbers of remote dependencies. Agents are much more efficient than RPCs, but they also require a greater infrastructure commonality than RPCs. Agents, unlike RPCs, can act similarly to Internet browser plug-ins. Given an application with a set of procedures available, third parties can write agents that take advantage of those procedures, thus extending the server application's feature set.

RPCs require tight coordination between client and service. The RPC-level agreements take place at the procedure level and must be very specific. Agent environments, on the other hand, act as generalized environments that can converse with any exposed application interfaces. Agents can coordinate activities between several remote applications without requiring further network transmissions.

The other infrastructure required of agents includes a language that can be used for agent interpretation, a communication facility for message passing, a transport facility for exchanging agents, a packaging facility for wrapping agents, and a set of security processes that verify an agent's source, authority, and other security parameters. To date, no standard has emerged for any of these areas, save transport, that can take advantage of existing protocols such as HTTP, TCP/IP, and SMTP. Packaging, security, and communications remain major areas of research for agent aficionados.

The language issue can be considered somewhat flexible in that almost any language could be adapted for use in mobile agent communications. Anything from LISP, C++, and SQL on the well-known front, to more obscure languages like Safe-Tcl, Python, or Obliq might be used. I would look for serious contention between Java and ActiveX on the agent language front over the next couple of years.

Remote Ending Accepted

Despite the lack of standards, agents exist as both commercial products and research projects. Some companies, like General Magic, have developed extensive experience with agents, including the development of a complete agent environment, Tabriz (formally Telescript), that is intended for widespread agentification of public networks and for the collaboration between publicly available information sources and personal digital assistants or PDAs.

Agents and remote programming offer a new way to view network applications. Eventually the communications between systems will exist as a swarm of very small processes on every computer doing a number of very small things while communicating with each other. Over the past decade or two, structured programming has taught every programmer how to break an application into manageable chunks, avoiding the rambling, stream-of-consciousness coding often referred to as spaghetti. Laying out this discipline has provided an advantageous contingency skill that could not be anticipated by Edward Yourdon as he nursed COBOL's unwieldy youth into structured maturity.

The joys of remote programming come in many forms. We can take our structured experience and move it onto the network, reducing network overhead while increasing server functionality and application flexibility. As a writer, I receive great joy thinking about the future of agents. The metaphors for teeming swarms of things scurrying around a network are much richer than the dry techno-babble of RPCs.

LOWERED EXPECTATIONS

After a few months' acquaintance with European "coffee,"
one's mind weakens, and his faith with it, and he begins to
wonder if the rich beverage of home, with its clotted layer
of yellow cream on top of it, is not a mere dream after all,
and a thing which never existed.
                                                —Mark Twain, *A Tramp Abroad*

AI runs rampant on the Web. Everywhere I look, I find pages screaming about intelligent agents. These agents search the Web, newsgroups, and other Internet resources for specific information and relay it, like happy puppies carrying slippers, to their masters. I have nothing against happy puppies, but I viewed AI as a more noble endeavor. Even as I have written about my doubts that AI will achieve its goals, I nonetheless respected the endeavor. The quest to mimic human intelligence in software and hardware was a search that, if nothing else, forced a closer examination of what makes us human.

I fear, that like many other intellectual pursuits, the Web's rapid ascension has changed everything. Intelligence is bantered about for tiny pieces of software that do little more than find changes in content and return pointers or download copies. This is not exactly rocket science. After watching Deep Blue defeat Gary Kasparov, I know that AI research continues along its traditional lines, but the perception is being diluted by the background murmurs of dozens of companies clamoring for "intelligence" mind share.

As with puppies, I like agents. I find intelligent agents extremely useful—not for their intelligence, but as a way to preserve my sanity through the onslaught of information thrown and strewn on the world's Web servers. There is too much of everything, including too much of the stuff I am really interested in. So agents, bots, whatever you want to call them, have an extremely important role in the management of information resources.

These agents, however, are far from intelligent. Their knowledge bases consist of Web-crawling methodologies driven by my parameters. Most of the agents lack even rudimentary intelligence such as semantic dictionaries to expand searches based on meanings or rule bases that support divergent searches based on conceptually related ideas.

I did not choose the quotation from Mr. Twain lightly. It certainly supports my assertion that Web agents water down AI, but it is also a quotation about coffee. The other threat to AI work comes from Java.

This Java Just Isn't My Brew

I was recently reading a Microelectronics and Computer Technology Corporation (MCC) paper by Nigel Jacobs and Ray Shea called "The Role of Java in InfoSleuth" (www.mcc.com/projects/infosleuth) and found that as Java makes its push as the universal executable on the Web, it is lowering our expectations of AI languages. It's just what we have to work with, say many Web *Meisters*. I for one, think the new language of choice has a few things to learn still from its older brethren.

InfoSleuth represents an extension to the earlier Carnot architecture that sought to bridge geographically distributed databases via a single semantic representation. InfoSleuth extends the database connection to any kind of distributed data that lacks central controls and changes rapidly. InfoSleuth implements a wide variety of cooperating agents that process queries, analyze data, mine knowledge, decompose queries, broker information, and format results. Much of InfoSleuth relies on Java as a platform-independent executable. InfoSleuth uses emerging AI standards such as the Knowledge Interchange Format, KIF and the Knowledge Query Language, KQML, for knowledge representation and sharing. These standards are joined by proprietary tools such as MCC's own LDL++ for deductive database systems and CLIPS, an old standby for expert-system research based on research at NASA.

I am not going to go further into the InfoSleuth architecture but focus on conclusions about Java. Java was great for heterogeneous execution. It is a good, robust, general-purpose language that supports multithreading, garbage collection, and strong compile-time type-checking.

OK, so Java is a good computer language. It is a good computer language for everything except learning systems. Java lacks a critical capability that is found in AI-oriented languages, like CLOS and in most expert-system products. Java does not support the dynamic creation of classes.

In most applications, the need to create classes on the fly means very little. Structured methodologies and good specifications eliminate the need to change because the application knows what it is going to do and it always does the same thing. Learning systems need the ability to adapt over time, and adaptation requires that basic values and beliefs be modified. The world changes so the meta-knowledge in a learning system must change.

Using Java for agents lowers expectations. It straight-jackets agents into predefined snippets of code rather than dynamic participants in an information ecology. MCC will use languages that do allow for a full range of class instantiation to interface with Java in order to provide those necessary dynamic functions. Internet agents written in Java will not have the advantage of MCC's experience, so they are not likely to miss a feature they never had.

The Internet and the Web present wonderful environments for the exploration of human knowledge. But as with any popular reflection of a sophisticated idea, the Web simplifies the details, smoothes the edges, and makes the reflection look better than the original, even if it is only a facade. AI will never be simple and the agents on the net will not be able to take full advantage of AI's contributions unless they interface with applications that support the full expressiveness of languages like CLOS.

Just One Final Cup

Even the most sophisticated agents perform very little reasoning. Agents are meant to live in communities, to negotiate, to barter, to share information, perhaps even to evolve from experience. The current literature about agents certainly does not preclude those capabilities, and even drives toward them. The Web, however, has become popular culture, and outside of William Gibson's Wintermute, AI has not fared well in popular culture.

As a AI aficionado, I almost yawned at Deep Blue. Rather impressive programming, but I could not ask Deep Blue how it felt after defeating Kasparov, I had to listen to its programmers to hear the thrill of victory and the hint of ego. Deep Blue raw powered its way into chess. It possessed no subtlety and no grace. It did one thing well and only that thing.

My final issue with agents is that they do only one thing well. Agents search only for what one tells them to search for. They are incapable of making grand leaps of illogic that connect oil spill clean up with gardening. And in their relentless logic, they will suffer many to settle into an ill-conceived comfort that agents are watching the important stuff. That all that should be known is known. So much stuff will squeeze through the agent filters that there may be little time for the recipient to look elsewhere for connections that lead down divergent allies, be they fruitful or not.

I still doubt our ability to create artificial intelligence in a computer sufficiently sophisticated that it will mimic us with little trace of its machine heritage. Machines will become intelligent, but in their own way and in their own time. Unfortunately the popularization of AI in intelligent agents my divert skilled researchers into commercial ventures bent on selling agent flotsam rather than concentrating on understanding how we think and how our thinking relates to our technology.

2

LEARNING FROM ARTIFICIAL INTELLIGENCE

AI and objects have common origins, but their popular acceptance came from different sources and at different times. Although the AI community always knew the power of hierarchical data constructions, the software world was many years behind in discovering this abstraction that both bring a more ordered appearance to data structures and help create a more common language between programmers and the users of computers.

WHAT CAN WE LEARN FROM AI?

AI used objects, or frames, because the intellectual truths of the time pegged us as animals of categorization. And indeed, if you sit in a room long enough with enough people and start talking about pretty much anything, some heated discussion will arise about what to call something and how that something is related to other things. We create classes and we are damn well going to defend them in public, even if no one has ever quite had our take on life.

The OO community can learn a great deal from AI, not on the programming level, but on the level of how to think about the programs themselves. OO people, for the most part, still think about objects as convenient repositories for procedural code. AI people think of objects as declarations of fact. A thing is and a thing does. As I have mentioned many times, objects make us anthropomorphize, even when we don't want to. And that, to me, is a good thing. The more we break the barriers between computer language and human language, the closer we come to creating applications that no longer need the translation.

And that translation, is itself, something OO can learn from AI. Object programming was sold as a way to modularize code so that it could be reused. It was sold for the economic benefit, not for the intellectual benefit. Well, I guess from the money being spent on OO these days, that camp certainly had the right idea when it comes to selling. But as a favorite boss tells me, we don't need to deceive, we just need to paint the picture the right way.

AI sold on the benefits of its applications to corporations and governments, but OO concentrated on selling MIS and programmers on the benefits of OO programming to them. Sure the corporations gained some benefit at the bottom line because programs were supposed to be delivered more efficiently in less time. What OO did not do was embrace other truths about the benefits of classes and instances, even if they just kept those truths to themselves.

In fact, many C++ or Java programmers have very little knowledge about the history of their languages or the history of programming. AI programs teach history, sometimes to a fault. I don't know one person in AI that doesn't know the story of MYCIN or half a dozen other anecdotes that don't help you pass finals, but are certainly required knowledge for polite conversation with other knowledge engineers.

With OO languages programmers tackle textbook problems and work algorithms; if they accidentally take an AI class to expand their horizons, they are often asked to switch gears and write in LISP or Prolog. Great languages, my favorites, but the connection between C++ and LISP is often lost on the student, and the techniques of that strange class never make it to the front line arsenal of coding techniques by the time the now ex-student lands a real job.

This chapter teaches some of the things that AI brings to the understanding of computer languages and problem solving. I don't go into game theory or alpha/beta pruning; you can check the reading list at the back of the book for those references. This chapter helps frame the discussion. It brings a bit of history and a bit of perspective. Most of all, I hope that those with a background in OO programming will take a few minutes to step out of the box and see new possibilities beyond the algorithm.

OBJECTS VS. FRAMES

Object-oriented knowledge-based tools confuse people—especially people with training in artificial intelligence. Many AI companies market their products as object oriented, but most of them do not possess the basic ingredients of objects. These tools are really frame-based. Frames, as you edit their data, look strikingly similar to objects, but both theoretical background and implementation differentiate them significantly. Objects and frames are converging, but that convergence may not be the best answer for objects or for frames—but alternatives exist.

A Framework for Frames

Frames were suggested in 1975 by Marvin Minsky, of MIT's Artificial Intelligence Laboratory, as a way of grouping knowledge in vision and natural language systems. Frames represent prototypical versions of events and things. If I walk into a living room, it takes me very little subjective time to identify a chair. Somewhere in my brain, Minsky theorizes, exists the prototype for a chair.

When presented with new data, the brain searches through its frames for the most likely match. These prototypes, however, have their limits. Confronted with a chair in the museum of modern art, the brain may wonder, to the point of becoming verbal: "What is that?" A few more cycles, however, identify the strange, misshapen object as a chair. Extensions to my frames occur naturally, so next time I encounter an avant-garde chair of similar style, it matches much more easily.

Expectations underlay the idea of frames. When you walk into a doctor's office, you expect certain things. Over the years, a prototype of visits to the doctor built up in your mind. You expect to be weighed and have your blood pressure and temperature taken.

Minsky described frames as a network of nodes and relationships. If you look at a frame system in graphic representation, it looks much like a nodal diagram or directed graph. High-level descriptions provide prototypes for actual occurrences. The actual doctor visit you made on October 28, 1992 contains several filled-in data elements. In the parlance of frames, these are known as slots.

At the very highest level, frames are a series of classes. The classes differentiate through two primary types of default relationships. KINDOF relationships describe specializations of classes into subclasses. The class of Begonias represents a specialization of the class FloweringPlants. DansBegonia ISA Begonia states the instance to class relationship. DansBegonia is the representation of an actual thing. Instances represent the lowest level things in a frame-based system.

Frames have a hierarchy of classes and instances that represent ideas and things in the real world. That sounds a lot like objects. The basic structures of these two electronic representations are indeed similar, but the use of the two and the details of their implementations make them very different.

The Object of Frames

Objects act and frames are acted upon. That is perhaps the largest difference between the two. Objects contain program layers that buffer the data within them from the outside world. Frames do not traditionally embody the idea of encapsulation. Frames act as internal memory structures for expert-system shells. The inference engine contained in an expert system reasons about frames. Objects, on the other hand, perform their own actions.

Frames do have procedural attachments, like methods, but they reside at the slot level, not the frame level. These attachments, called *demons*, often go by the names of WHEN-NEEDED or BEFORE-CHANGED and AFTER-CHANGED.

- WHEN-NEEDED demons execute at the time a slot value is required for an inference. The procedure establishes a series of actions that the system should take to obtain a value. Typically, a default value is established when all other sources fail. Sophisticated expert systems use SQL links to gather data from SQL compliant databases. The WHEN-NEEDED slot, in this case, would contain instructions for how to get a value from an SQL table on a database server.

- BEFORE-CHANGED demons execute before a slot value changes. These actions often set-up the system for subsequent reaction to a new value. The idea of non-monotonic reasoning relies on a system's ability to reorient itself based on new information. The BEFORE-CHANGED method could reset certain values, based on the incoming value, thus forcing the inference engine to rethink something that moments ago it knew to be fact.

- ☑ AFTER-CHANGED methods facilitate reaction to a change in the expert system's world. Once a value changes, other things may be logically required. Expert systems are used to monitor sensors in process control applications. If sensor reading suddenly changes to reflect danger, it is the AFTER-CHANGED method that most likely triggers the shut down of critical systems.

Keeping related frames in sync is another common task for the AFTER-CHANGE demon. If I buy a particular TV, it becomes an item in my property slot. At the same time, the ownership for the TV should change from The Good Feds Department Store, to Dan Rasmus.

In addition to the procedural attachments, a slot usually contains constraints and other information for a slot, such as prompts, allowable values, and data type. The collection of all information about a slot is referred to as a *facet*.

Software objects profess to be complete microcosmic programs. If you ask an object to display itself, an invoked method displays a bit-mapped image. Although it is possible for a frame to act in the same fashion, the action would occur from within the inference engine, not from within the frame itself. A statement like: DISPLAY "BITMAP1" in the AFTER-CHANGE demon of a frame would certainly display a bitmap. The bitmap display procedure, however, exists not in the frame, but in the basic code of the expert-system shell.

Objects have a much richer set of methods than do frames. Anything you can write as a program can become an object method. Message passing allows a wide variety of interactions between objects, something that frames do not facilitate in the same manner. Some frame systems now implement object-like message passing, but this moves them more toward the object paradigm and away from pure frame knowledge representation.

Object-oriented systems constrain their inheritance structures to simple ISA and KINDOF relationships. These form the basis of frame structures as well, but frame systems, like Carnegie Group's KnowledgeCraft, add several default relationships like Part-of, Has-Parts, Set,

Subset, Member-of, Next-to, Subsumes, and Reports-to. User defined relationships are common in high-end frame systems. Not all of these relationships require inheritance—they act as ways of adding details and granularity to the knowledge base that make it more computationally expressive.

The implementation of frames and objects come from very different places. Although the similarities exist, the philosophy behind the two are very different. Object-oriented practitioners view the world as buttons, menus, and automated guided vehicles in virtual worlds—the representation and behavior of software objects. Knowledge engineers view frames as the knowledge structure over which their systems match prototypes and reason. Objects are a technique and frames are a philosophy. When working with groups destined to implement knowledge in software, I often suggest they read Hume and Russell long before they concentrate on Booch, Meyer, or Coad/Yourdan.

The Problem with Frames

Frames, as described by Minsky, create walls through which AI researchers must go. The largest of frame systems to date exists in the form of CYC, the commonsense knowledge base project at Austin's Microelectronics and Computer Technology Corporation (MCC). Doug Lenat and his team have created the world's largest knowledge base, built tacitly around the idea of frames.

As CYC grew, the team found limits to the framework of frames. Frames do not take kindly to negation. A platypus is a mammal, but it isn't a typical mammal. Frames make a relationship like (platypus ISNOT typical mammal) difficult to represent. Although a platypus certainly belongs in the class of mammals, so many of the defaults fail to adequately describe its physiology or behavior that hand building a new platypus frame takes less time than cutting off the default value inheritance.

Frames force implementers, therefore, to look at typical cases. Arguably 99.9 percent of all telephones have keys for 0, 1, 2, 3, 4, 5, 6, 7, 8, and 9. Frames would force you to represent all telephones and all numbers attached to them if you wanted to capture that rare case where a telephone was missing the 7 key. This .1 percent chance may have no significance in your system, so you abstract around it by assuming all telephones are whole. If you need, however, to reason about a broken telephone, frames make it difficult to capture the idea: all telephones have 10 number keys (ranging from 0 to 9) with the exception of phone 13245870, which is missing the 7 key.

The CYC solution to this problem involves melding a predicate logic-based constraint language over the frame structure. The system then handles the translations between logical statements and the lower-level representation. This does not solve the need for very detailed frames, but it does buffer knowledge engineers from the creation of the lower-level representations.

CYC goes beyond conventional frame wisdom to make descriptions of slot frames as well. This internal descriptor allows CYCalists to create complex constraints about slots, create relationships between slots (beyond relationships between frames), and reason about the structure of CYC's world. CYC, therefore, given the right constraints and knowledge about the world, would conclude that it was impossible for my daughter Rachel to work in space because she is not an astronaut. In this case, the slots for occupation and geographic location of occupation are related and constrained by each other.

For systems not as ambitious as CYC, frames work. Even in CYC, frames represent the core structure of its underlying knowledge. Frames are simple to implement and are computationally efficient. Doug Lenat states, "A large fraction of what we want to represent can quite naturally be expressed in u[nit].s[lot].v[alue] triples. This being the case, it is computationally useful to have a well-defined, simple language that is sufficient for that large number of cases. In other words, the frame language is more efficient, so let's use it whenever we can."

The Question of GUIs

Many of the commercial AI companies have cluttered their knowledge space with GUI derivatives. I become distracted from the knowledge I want to capture by the constant reminder I am creating a production system. The companies with frames and no objects concentrate their efforts on linking slot values to GUI widgets. A gauge, for instance, moves as a slot value changes. This is fine, but the GUI widget becomes an instance in my local knowledge base that has nothing to do with the knowledge about how the value changes.

Objects clearly represent graphic items better than frames. Graphic items, by their very nature, are software objects. They need information about screen coordinates, what they should look like, and how they should behave when clicked on. Message passing acts as a wonderful metaphor for communication between GUI objects. None of those things means anything in a knowledge base.

Ideal systems combine the talents of several software traditions, but they should partition the environments between knowledge implementation or interface implementation. Neuron Data and their Nexpert Object product are often derided because Nexpert lacks interface building capabilities. With the next release of Nexpert, Neuron Data will combine Nexpert with their Open Interface (OI) GUI development tools.

Although the tools will exist within the same shell and be completely interactive, the majority of information about the configuration of the GUI elements remains in the OI memory partition. The links between slot values and the GUI happen in OI, not in Nexpert. Nexpert's interaction with OI takes the form of control. When a rule concludes that a user needs information, a window is called. Custom input dialogs and windows are also callable from Nexpert, but the knowledge engineer need only know the names of the windows, not the details of their constituent parts.

GUI developers using objects can learn much from their knowledge engineering counterparts. Knowledge engineers study classification schemes as part of their training, most software engineers do not. Knowledge engineers must maintain large systems with many related frames. Reuse of software requires the same strong semantic organization as frame-based expert systems. This organization may not come readily to early adopters of the technology. Teaming with knowledge engineers to help determine names and linkages between object classes can go a long way toward achieving reuse goals.

Many expert systems use frames to mimic GUI interface objects, but this adds greatly to the complexity of the dialog between the knowledge engineer and the expert system. Knowledge engineers, assigned to create total systems, like the rapid prototyping capabilities found in these tools. In the next section I suggest an alternative approach to the evolution of frames into objects.

An Intelligent Object Architecture

Perhaps the best way to solve the potential conflicts between objects and frames involves creating intelligent objects. Current frame-based systems rely on an expert-system shell and programming environment. The frames themselves, even with demons attached, act only within the functions of the system in which they reside. Even LISP-based tools require you to drop out of the expert system and write an occasional function in LISP—C-based tools often require call-outs to C routines. Expert systems are not computationally complete.

Objects systems, on the other hand, are capable of creating new environments and new systems. Nexpert Object and Kappa are written in C. A compilable object system could incorporate the basics of Nexpert or Kappa as methods of a class called ThingsThat-Think.

ThingsThatThink includes methods for rule development, frame development, debugging, inferencing, and other expert systems standards. Objects attached to this class would contain slots of data-type Knowledge. The individual knowledge bases, rather than being separate files, would be binary data inside the object. When an object required an internal decision, it would use a rule set differentiator to determine which rule set to submit to the inference method. The differentiator could be so simple that the arguments passed to it could determine the rule set.

If you created a printed circuit board repair object, the system would contain rules for electrical repairs (capacitors, ICs, and resistors) and mechanical repairs (cables and connectors). The object might receive a message from the test method that says: Short at R2. The method differentiator recognizing that a short is an electrical failure, loads the electrical rule set. The inference session then diagnoses the situation, asks other methods or the end user for more information if needed, and prescribes a solution.

In a pure object-oriented environment, the implementors of this idea would probably create rule objects, frame objects, and relationship objects that represent the representations. The way an object-oriented system programmer implements this idea is unimportant to the knowledge engineer.

An inference engine is, after all, just a class of program. Objects and their methods are tools for building programs. Their conflict needs to exist between the two paradigms. The current solutions converge on one answer: extend frames to resemble objects. This answer muddles the real needs of both worlds. People building user interfaces and procedural programs must maintain unnecessary overhead for such things as slot procedure attachments. Knowledge engineers, on the other hand, become distracted from their primary task—knowledge representation.

The architecture suggested above provides the object-oriented system builders with a non-interference policy. The inference engine and other knowledge engineering tools become methods. The knowledge engineer is also happy, as long as the methods provide the expected functionality.

The Object of It All

Frames provide knowledge engineers with expressive and functional ways of representing knowledge from their human experts. Frames do not contain the constructive power of objects and they should not. Their purpose should stop where the line blurs. Objects do a better job of constructing overall systems, so they should be left to that end. The two software communities need to negotiate toward a standard interaction. When the marriage of these two worlds works successfully, we may see why neither paradigm was as productive apart as they are together. I look forward to working in future environments where the objects are capable of capturing knowledge and where knowledge becomes an integral part of every software system.

WHAT MORE CAN WE LEARN FROM AI?

Not all AI research focuses on how to make machines think. A significant portion of research deals with how people think and how to organize knowledge. As the 1990s mature, corporate systems will require higher and higher levels of knowledge. They will not necessarily be intelligent; they will, however, be organized intelligently and deliver software that leverages the expertise of the enterprise.

Lessons learned in AI can help object-oriented practitioners organize their classes, add inferencing to objects, and help developers get capture-and-retain business knowledge.

Organization

As I watch people create new classes in Smalltalk, C++, Eiffel, and other languages, I wonder how much thought goes into the taxonomy of the class structure. In AI, the names assigned to frames, to steal from T.S. Eliot, aren't "just one of your everyday names." Frames derive from a theory of human knowledge organization. They are not simply nuggets of code available for reuse. They are nuggets of knowledge that should be easily found and easily navigated.

The growth of classes presents major problems for developers. "How do I know if someone has already done that?" "Now what class was that blankity-blank method attached to?" Ever heard questions like that before?

Most IS shops apply a very strict rule to software development: Everybody for him-/herself. Objects do not attempt to modify that thought process. The organization of material is a conscious decision. No available software development technology organizes material without human intervention. Objects should be viewed not as software components, but as business process components. They represent significant corporate value and must be managed like people, inventory, and cash flow. (Eventually we can hope that intelligent cataloging software will find the code for us when we ask— stay tuned.)

To leverage your object investment, invest in new skills. Linguistics, semantics, knowledge engineering, and cognitive psychology now play a role in software development. Not in your shop, you say? If they do not, the organization of your object libraries is likely less than optimal, and your software is more likely focused on software developer issues than a broader human context. COBOL and FORTRAN forced artificial processes to interact with organic processes. With objects, we return to organic thinking.

Software objects fall into two main categories: Software engineering components and components that represent real things. The software engineering components should reflect a general order because developers defined the world within which the objects exist. User interface layout objects mean nothing to an inventory control clerk. Asking that person to create intuitive information groupings would result in missing information and suboptimal applications.

Ask an inventory control person to organize their knowledge and you will likely get a more reasoned result. Ask him or her about parts and vendors, delivery and inventory picking processes. The world of inventory is his or her domain at least eight hours a day. The person consummated an organization through experience and industry interaction that no programmer can hope to achieve in the inventory control domain. They can describe and order the information by applying their knowledge. They need know nothing of the actual implementation.

What does an object-oriented programmer do with inventory knowledge when confronted with a new inventory module? Treats it like a software project, right? What they should do is work with skilled knowledge engineers (or better yet, become one themselves) to organize the data in such a way that it is intuitive to the customer of the system.

Classes and their objects should represent knowledge about the world as seen by the person who owns the domain knowledge. Software engineers will tend to break up that knowledge into different schemes. Where an inventory control person would refer to an inventory location as the relationship between a part and a physical bin at certain coordinates, the software engineer might construct location as an alphanumeric attribute of part.

By defining the richer model, it would be possible to model the area, rather than just code it. A stockroom model populated with inventory and inventory locations can be queried about location contents, and parts can rely on their whereabouts. Both can know the quantity in each other. It would also be possible, in this construction, to create a visual representation of the warehouse.

AI can teach us about organization and provide for more flexible representations of our physical and mental worlds. Our objects should reflect the knowledge structure of the people whose expertise we gather. We are not necessarily dealing with the depth of knowledge AI attempts, but we are dealing with a higher order of knowledge than that found in non-object-oriented systems. The very nature of objects lends itself to a more organic architecture. But an organization of knowledge would be incomplete without the knowledge itself. The next thing we learn from AI is how to acquire that knowledge.

Knowledge Acquisition

Most programmers are concerned with algorithms. We recode complex tax calculations or inventory-netting formulas and find clever ways to optimize working memory, disk storage, and CPU. The knowledge we code is transparent and recordable. Most of the time this knowledge limits itself to a few, if any, options and variations. When the knowledge changes, as in the case of payroll deductions, the instructions are documented and communicated in great detail.

As we add more knowledge into our software, the systems analyst will need to adopt new methods for capturing, documenting, and retrieving knowledge. Our current applications successfully emulate categorization knowledge, clerical knowledge, and calculation knowledge. Outside of the smallest companies, it is unlikely you will find any place in America where payroll check calculations take place manually. Even in the smallest companies PC and spreadsheet systems take the gross income and spread it around to various federal, state, and local vultures.

But there are knowledge areas within a corporation untouched by automation. Two of these are readily apparent to even the most closeted of MIS professionals: the help desk and management. Automate management, you ask? My answer is why not?

Managers spend much of their time making simple decisions that require readily accessible data (should you decide to make it readily accessible, that is). Let me give you an example. A new project comes up. Who is the best person or people to work on that project? The manager checks project logs, looks for available resources, checks on skills, and makes assignments. Easily automatable, huh? What project logs does one check? How are resource skills defined? Do people know things outside the skills profiles? There are visible answers to these questions and invisible answers to these questions. The knowledge engineer attacks the invisible answers.

Before we move on to knowledge engineering in detail, return to the help desk. Like the manager, the help desk is a function composed of documented information, such as the troubleshooting guide at the end of a software manual. It also has a hidden component, the experiential knowledge of the people helping other people.

Both of these applications and thousands of others require the poking, prodding, and enticing of knowledge engineering. Algorithms will not make up the bulk of 1990–2000 programming. Rules, facts, and object structures will replace the clarity of the known, with the fuzziness of the vague.

As knowledge engineers know, not only do most people not know what they know, they don't explain what they do know they know very well.

Declarative Knowledge

If you are discussing the physical appearance of the people at the table next to you and you point out that the woman's dress is blue, you have transmitted declarative knowledge. Declarative knowledge is the easiest type of knowledge to gather; it is also the least useful. If you are trying to find out how someone does something, you will have to extract procedural knowledge. Declarative knowledge provides you with the color and texture of your domain. If you are going to represent knowledge in an object-oriented fashion, then the declarative knowledge you gather will provide the first-level description of the world.

Procedural Knowledge

Procedural knowledge retains the step-by-step procedures used to do things. Much of AI's success comes from distributing this "how-to" knowledge throughout an organization. The actions taken to validate timecards, to fix a printer jam, or to deposit a check involve the execution of procedures. Some procedures are very easy to capture; others, like how to shut down a nuclear reactor, are difficult and complex.

Semantic Knowledge

Semantic knowledge constitutes our deepest levels of understanding and proves the most difficult to capture. Knowledge engineers spend hours digging into the recesses of an expert's mind. Semantic knowledge is a pool of concepts and intertwined relationships. The validity and usefulness of non-procedural projects will rely on your team's skill with semantic knowledge gathering.

Episodic Knowledge

Some of your knowledge about the world is not gained through long study of specific facts or even on the synthesis of facts and their relationships with other facts. Think of an expert baker or expert driver. How much does the baker think when mixing a recipe? Think about your wandering mind as you drive. The activities of driving or creating a soufflé associate with space and time—you recall them in a mental play. You get to work not because you *procedured* the drive, but because you replayed it. Episodic knowledge proves difficult to recognize and capture because of its personal nature and the tendency for it to interconnect with semantic knowledge until the two virtually merge.

Table 2.1: Acquisition Techniques for Teasing Knowledge Types from an Expert

Knowledge Type	Acquisition Techniques
Declarative	Concept sorting Inferential flow analysis Repertory grid Multidimensional scaling
Semantic	Concept sorting Scenarios Inferential flow analysis Repertory grid
Procedural	Interviewing Observation Protocol analysis Scenarios Decision analysis
Episodic	Interviewing Protocol analysis Task analysis Scenarios Event recall

Forgetting What We Know

Experts, being human, don't store knowledge in a way that is easily accessed by other humans. People with a wide knowledge of a subject and many years of experience will have knowledge of many types about their subject. Small chucks of knowledge have changed internal representations over the years and become related to other pieces of information learned at other times. That is why we forget what we know. We still know it. We might even remember learning it, but mental reorganizations changed the pointers. Now rather than thinking, we do. If you doubt that statement, dial a phone and try to explain to your son or daughter how you did it. Not just pushing the buttons, but the mental processes you engaged to push them. You'll find it easier to explain VCR programming to your mother-in-law than phone dialing to your kids.

In the business world, teasing knowledge out of people is crucial. People represent the business. What they do and how they do it makes the business function. In the past, centralized knowledge represented power. Now it represents costs. The move in most companies is distributed, team-based decisions. Individuals with knowledge bottleneck processes and increase costs. With software, we can capture much of that knowledge and distribute it on our networks.

Concept Sorting

When you become familiar with a domain, you will put together a dictionary of sorts that represents the concepts of the domain. In manufacturing cars you may gather an assortment of concepts like:

Frame
    Door
    Weld
Rework
    Paint
    Robot
Mean-time-between failures
Parts-per-million
Quality
    Test
Quality ASSURANCE
Receiving inspection

This list represents the beginnings of a concepts list for car manufacturing. In concept sorting you take this type of list and place each word on a 3×5 card (or you use a visual outliner/mind mapper on a computer, like Inspiration Software's "Inspiration") and ask the expert to sort the concepts according to a category. Some of the words will become super-concepts because they embody several other concepts. Quality would be an example of a super-concept because it includes the concepts of mean-time-between failures, parts-per-million, test and quality assurance. Concepts can appear in more than one place in the hierarchy.

The relationships between the words in concept sorting are more important than the words themselves. Concept sorting is a way to establish a framework for the knowledge engineering task. By working through the concepts you can identify ideas that were missed, and eliminate areas that do not appear to fit within the project's scope. Concepts sorting, although not as natural as interviewing, is a good way to start a project because it helps both the knowledge engineer and the expert clarify their thinking. Rules will not result from concept sorting, but declarative knowledge and semantic knowledge are common outputs of a concept sorting effort. It proves an apt starting place for the organization of objects and their methods.

Is That It?

The organization of knowledge and the techniques for gathering knowledge are perhaps the two most evident influences AI can make on objects, but here are a few more thoughts to consider.

Inference algorithms exist in droves. Learn and implement these; do not create your own. You should strive to create a robust and flexible set of methods that handle forward chaining, backward chaining, theorem proving, and other algorithms. Some other inferencing methods, such as searching trees of represented knowledge, come easier to objects than to AI.

With the common inferencing, you will establish standard ways of representing knowledge in rules and objects. One of the failures of commercial AI was the lack of interoperable standards. Outside of a couple of public domain representations like OPS5 and its cousin, CLIPS from NASA, commercial AI suppliers force you to buy the company along with the product. In this age of interchangeable code, a set of routines common to all systems will make AI more appealing as a value-added cost in your applications development efforts.

Since knowledge doesn't port from package to package, AI suppliers created links to databases and other applications. They also learned, as the client/server world is learning, that the world is heterogeneous. Companies like Neuron Data delivered interoperable versions of their products on almost every conceivable piece of hardware. Today Neuron leverages that expertise in their client/server tools called Smart Elements.

Still Much To Learn

Gathering and distributing knowledge presents the most profound difficulty for IS professionals over the next few years. The demand for intelligent software grows everyday. The business community is tired of conforming to the restrictions placed on them by IS. They want systems that spread expertise throughout the organization. The hybrid analyst-programmer-knowledge engineer of the '90s will need to build on the techniques and experience of diverse disciplines, including AI.

AI failed to make a major impact on its own because its promises were ahead of its ability to deliver. We are much closer now to delivering on the technology promises of AI. Although technology exists to capture corporate knowledge, retain corporate memory, and distribute expertise, the difficulties of teasing that knowledge from the business community remains. If we don't make conscious efforts to reuse business knowledge, objects will become little more than software conveniences. Objects can leverage the expertise of programmers and the business. The successful implementation of both types of expertise depends on recognizing the impact of people, thought, and mental organization—not just technology.

There is much the object-oriented community can learn from AI. Subsequent parts of this book will explore many other areas of interaction between objects and AI.

INTELLIGENT INFORMATION ENGINEERING

Information engineering (IE) was devised to bring information technology closer to the business. Information engineering captures the hopes and desires of the executive office and links them intimately to requirements for information systems. At least in theory. Several companies use information engineering for planning, but few realize its potential to guide development from concept to code.

Information engineering evolved in the 1970s and 1980s around databases and terminals. New technologies like knowledge-based systems, distributed computing, and objects are not found in the popular texts on IE. The lack of integration makes IE difficult to adopt in forward-thinking software shops. But like all methodologies, IE works best when it is modified to meet the needs of the company and situation. This section will provide one view of how distributed computing, knowledge-based systems, and objects fit into the information engineering framework.

What Is Information Engineering?

Information Engineering encompasses a womb-to-tomb philosophy of information technology. Rather than just gather user requirements and crank out code, IE attempts to link every phase of the development process to business strategies and goals. IE is about architectures.

Imagine your information systems shop as a bougainvillea clutching the side of your house. Without a trellis it will soon collapse and sprawl across your pansies. Most IS shops today were created without a concern for support infrastructure. Business believed in the computer's intrinsic ability to solve problems. The computer accelerated both the right and the wrong. New automation created new bottlenecks as previously adequate manual processes tried to meet the demand of automation upstream. In some cases, automating existing manual processes just generated mistakes and misinformation more swiftly.

Information engineering creates a framework for the implementation of technology, applications, and data. If you need to automate a process, you go to the architecture and see how it connects to other processes and to data. You also check to see if it is already implemented somewhere else. Only if you can't find an existing solution to automating the process do you construct it. Processes must fit within the context of the architecture. IE creates a common environment for definitions of data and processes.

The process of information engineering is broken down into four main areas: Information Systems Planning (ISP), Business Area Analysis (BAA), Business System Design (BSD), and Business System

Construction (BSC). ISP differentiates information engineering from older methodologies by focusing on business, not code. IE continuously reassesses the business relevance of automated solutions. Lower levels of IE appear to do little more than tie together and tighten already existing methodologies and techniques like entity-relationship diagramming, structured systems analysis, and function analysis. Unlike those techniques, IE integrates the techniques with their business rationale.

There's Engineering; Then There's Engineering

IE is as close to traditional engineering as anything introduced to information systems. Many companies, from IBM to Texas Instruments, have found information engineering strategic to their business. Current descriptions and implementations of information engineering, however, are oriented toward terminals and databases. The methodology does not ask questions that lead to answers like CD-ROM, expert system, or distributed computing. Even if it did, the mechanisms for building those systems are not integral to IE.

Some commercial IE texts acknowledge new technologies by adding a step here or there. Most versions of IE identify needed technologies, but few do anything to support the development of systems that use them. We will address the technical problems with IE later (see "Concurrent Engineering" later in this chapter).

The lack of support for new technologies is not IE's only Achilles' heel—it also suffers from long lead-time expectations. Depending on the size of the company, it might take a year or two to create a useful architecture. The architecture's enterprise level view of business strategies, data, and processes provides value to IE, not its detailed methods like data flow diagramming. The comprehensive view of information in an architecture creates the context for applying lower level techniques. Without an architecture, random reaction, rather than plans derived from the architecture, drive the system's development process.

Information systems departments are often ill equipped to take on multi-year projects. In our quick gratification society, a report tomorrow morning is more important than an architecture next month or next year. The fault is not one of method, but one of perception. Without an appreciation for the future, the tricks of history replay themselves. An IE architecture maps the data, processes, and technologies required to achieve strategic goals. Companies that pay attention to today's details in lieu of strategy may never reach their goals.

The Information Strategic Planning (ISP) phase alone helps produce a synergy between the operating community and the information technology community. It is, however, the everyday use of the architecture that makes it important. Each time it is used to populate new data or implement a new process, it also changes. Subtle and dramatic changes introduce themselves as the architecture is explored and implemented. Each phase adds new details and perspectives.

The information engineering methodology needs to grow as much as the architectures it generates. Even with its lack of support for new technologies, IE will support many planned and future projects with little modification. The data and processes required by the organization remain constant, even in the wake of new technologies. Technology adds the question "how do we implement it?" The question of "what do we implement?" remains the same.

Methodologies, unlike software, do not readily avail themselves to rapid updates. The research, development, and book publishing cycle is much slower than the software publishing cycle (at least most of the time). Old methodologies persist in the wake of overwhelming technological changes. New takes on IE and synthesis from within will yield a workable method that supports both information and technology planning.

Knowledge and Objects

A recent attempt by James Martin and James Odell to create object versions of information engineering (*Object-Oriented Analysis and Design*, Prentice Hall, 1992) fall short of the mark. Instead of integrating the whole of information technology, their methodology focuses on objects and ignores both old technologies and other new technologies. The modified methodology represents message passing, but not the links between an object and a mainframe database.

As knowledge engineers and object aficionados, it is important to understand how information engineering can help point to and justify the use of new technologies. The problem with integration, however, is not wholly placed with the gurus of information engineering.

Much of the problem stems from objects and knowledge-based systems themselves.

Although most of you reading this section will profess to some firsthand experience with knowledge engineering, few of you could agree on the concepts and tasks associated with it. Intellectual definitions of knowledge engineering exist, but practitioner perceptions differ greatly. Engineering a new product usually requires the execution of a set series of steps. Knowledge engineering is much more like laboratory prototyping or original research—it is more magic than science. Objects have a much more structured origin and will, as Martin and Odell aptly illustrate, lend themselves better to the structured world of IE.

Despite difficulties, major portions of what we can agree to assign the label "knowledge engineering" will fit within the IE framework. Rules become implementations of processes. Frames and cases become definitions of data. Repertory grids, protocol analysis, interviewing, and other techniques in KE supplement the techniques of traditional procedural programming and analysis.

Concurrent Engineering

In his book, *Information Engineering (Book I Introduction)*, [Prentice Hall, 1989], James Martin makes the following statement about expert systems:

- Information Engineering should use expert system techniques to help planners, analysts, and designers create better systems.

- Information engineering attempts to integrate these eight trends and to create one encyclopedia that relates to all the trends.

Unfortunately, this is the only place expert systems are mentioned in the book. There is no discussion of how to integrate them with IE—and this passage relates not to building expert systems, but to using them to build conventional systems. In another Martin book, *Building Expert Systems* (Prentice Hall, 1988), Martin and Steven Oxman describe a high-level view of expert systems development. Unfortunately, they do not mention IE once.

Today's systems planners, analysts, and builders need to find synergy between the diverse methods and techniques found in the knowledge engineering, object-oriented analysis and design, case-based reasoning.

Information Strategy Planning

The ISP phase of IE should identify strategic company knowledge in addition to capturing goals, strategies, and critical success factors. The analysis should focus on the knowledge that differentiates your company from others. The tactical plan deliverable should include new technologies and direction about how they should be used. Without including a strong direction from the top, most IS people will be content with the tools and languages they are familiar with.

Business Area Analysis

The business area analysis (BAA) phase is where knowledge actually comes into play. Analysts should identify candidate processes for knowledge-based systems. Processes that focus on decisions, retrieval of information, or analysis of information are ideal candidates for KBS development. Depending on the project, prototypes may be used during BAA to enhance and validate the requirements.

Distributed applications add another dimension to business area analysis. In addition to the detailed data, the dimension of location should be introduced. Location applies to both data and processes. Location data should also reflect the type of distribution, such as subsets of data or replicated data. This information will help distributed system designers, including those working on client/server applications, to determine which components should be placed on the client workstation, and how the data and processes should be distributed.

Business Systems Design

The design phase presents the first major hurdle to integration because the tools and techniques don't lend themselves to integration. Prior phases add whole items, or items that are derivative of other items (for example, life-cycle diagrams and even schemas).

Current IE tools do not capture knowledge explicitly. Knowledge and other design elements like methods, demons, explanations, and so forth must be captured outside the IE repository. They should, however, be developed with, and within, full sight of the total system design.

BSD logically contains knowledge acquisition techniques. Since this is a methodology, rules for applying techniques should be stated. Here is an example of how knowledge acquisition techniques might be applied based on knowledge type:

Declarative
Concept sorting
Inferential flow analysis
Repertory grid
Multidimensional scaling

Semantic
Concept sorting
Scenarios
Inferential flow analysis
Repertory grid

Procedural
Interviewing
Observation
Protocol analysis
Task analysis
Scenarios
Decision analysis

Episodic
Interviewing
Protocol analysis
Task analysis
Scenarios
Event recall

The BSD phase should also capture the logic flow of the system, including the logic of rules. Because of the introduction of new technologies, the diagramming techniques represented by IE fail to capture the new data.

Business Systems Construction

Construction of knowledge-based systems, distributed systems, or object-oriented systems remains essentially the same as construction in traditional systems. The problem during construction is one of integration. Most automated construction and testing tools focus on procedural languages like COBOL, FORTRAN, or C. There are no automated methods, or even well-documented manual methods, for integrated testing of a distributed intelligent object-oriented accounts payable system.

A few preliminary migration strategies will help move IE toward new technologies. Where possible, knowledge-based tools should have application programming interfaces (APIs) or libraries. With enterprise-level systems, reading and writing of database files from stand-alone tools is not adequate for most applications. Rather than complex schemes to pass data from a knowledge-based system to a traditional application, the knowledge-based system logic resides inside the application, callable as needed.

The ideal situation would be to treat everything as an object. The non-object-oriented technologies would be encapsulated by interface objects. This could be true for relational databases as well as knowledge-based systems. Because knowledge-based systems can't be checked algorithmically, they require intensive user involvement to verify the outcome of inferences. The user involvement should come early in the project and be maintained throughout construction.

Distributed computing requires clear strategies for the distribution of data and processes between nodes, and between physical clients and servers. The strategies should draw distinctions between shared data and local data and include how to deal with integrity concerns. If programmers know where data resides, they can enforce integrity rules and institute mechanisms to keep the data in synchronization. Eventually technology will resolve the issue of distributed data, but new solutions like those found in Oracle 7 remain proprietary.

Even the integration of knowledge engineering, object-oriented analysis, and design and information engineering does little if management is not in tune with the methodology. Much that we say about the adoption of knowledge-based systems is true of information engineering. Both require a visible, high-level commitment to the process. Both are expensive and require funding to match rhetoric.

Expanding Our Horizons

It is easy to focus on what you do and forget that other technologies and disciplines exist. As much as we would like to see knowledge engineering recognized as a legitimate business tool, it may not find its place without turning to client/server and object-oriented programming for assistance.

Object-oriented and client/server technology recently replaced AI as the main marketing thrust at many "AI" companies. Neuron Data entered the graphical user interface market with Open Interface, their object-oriented GUI builder. New versions of Nexpert will include Open Interface integrated with Nexpert. IntelliCorp shifted focus from its aging KEE expert system shell to client/server computing and objects with Kappa and ProKappa. Even stalwart OPS protector, Inference, recently announced an object-oriented, client/server "enterprise" product based on ART.

Neuron Data and IntelliCorp have strong ties to the information engineering community. Nexpert Object and ProKappa support third-party links to information engineering models created in KnowledgeWare's Application Development Workbench. ProKappa will soon ship as an executable CASE environment, where models of the business become applications.

The differences between knowledge engineering and traditional software development will narrow. As applications become more sophisticated, users will expect them to be more knowledgeable. The demand for competitive products with reasoning capability will force methodology developers to recognize the need for knowledge acquisition, knowledge documentation, and integrated testing of both knowledge and traditional computing elements.

The future of business computing lies in coupling it with strategic goals of the corporation. The choices of technology will only grow in complexity. Some will merge and new ones will evolve. Methods must rapidly adapt to the changing technology landscape. For corporations to take advantage of the new technologies, their structure and intentions must be supportive of innovation.

If methods do not move fast enough to support strategic goals, then corporations must enhance the methodology themselves. The practitioner should never be placed in the situation of using second-best technology because policies and procedures do not yet allow him or her to take advantage of an opportunity.

THINKING ABOUT OBJECTS

C++ is all the rage. But C++ is a programming language. Sure it allows you to create wonderfully object-oriented applications, but it still feels like programming. Compile and link. Debug. CLOS opens the doors to object-oriented software craftsmanship with its pliable interactivity. But CLOS is still LISP and only the backward thinking or forward thinking consider LISP. Eiffel, Smalltalk, and a host of other programming languages line up to compete for your software affections. But like C++ and CLOS, all of these options require serious study and an intimate knowledge of pointers, toolboxes, or class browsing.

There is an alternative. Well, several alternatives. The AI community has exploited the power of objects longer than most. AI objects parade different banners than those trumpeted by the traditional language folks, but they come with the same benefits: reusability, modularity, maintainability, understandable models, distribution, and a host of other, less well-agreed-to benefits. Knowledge-based system (KBS) products—known through the '70s and '80s—and expert-system shells have matured into object-oriented client/server development tools. Most of the vendors play down their AI roots in favor of the new business words of enterprise, client/server, and object-oriented.

An Object Lesson

The objects of AI were, and are, different than the objects of object-oriented programming. But they are getting closer. AI objects used to be called frames and were designed to organize and represent knowledge—in particular, the tangibles and intangibles of the real world. Objects, on the other hand, were conceived as extensions to software engineering that made coding easier. Eventually the two camps saw their similarities. It was the AI group that changed. The AI frame gave way to the first class object.

Unlike pure object-oriented languages, knowledge-based systems are not made exclusively of frames. They also contain rules. Rules exist at a higher order than objects in a knowledge-based system environment. Rules reason about objects. Above the rules sits the inference engine, which controls the action. Unlike object environments where everything must be coded or stolen from previous work, knowledge-based systems contain the high-level functionality of inference. They already know how to reason. It is the knowledge engineer's job to tell them what to reason about.

Rules may also act as methods. Most object-oriented KBS product support several ways to create a method. Methods may consist of rules; routines-written in the internal language; external routines; and, for older products written in LISP, LISP-functions. The combination of objects and inference methods create what the AI industry calls *hybrid systems*.

State-of-the-Object

Most of the high-end knowledge-based system development environments support objects. IntelliCorp's KappaPC and ProKappa, Platinum's Aion DS, and Brightware's ART*Enterprise all contain variations on the object theme. Nexpert Object 3.0, when it is released, will extend its frame orientation to include methods and message passing.

Rapid, incremental development environments remain the primary selling point for commercial knowledge-based system products. Gone are the hard-sell days of knowledge capture and thinking machines. Today's salesmen tout rapid development of client/server systems, easy access to corporate data, and prototypes that become full applications. Trinzic is so committed to client/server computing and corporate data access that they recently purchased Channel Computing and their Forest & Trees and InfoPump product lines. (Trinzic was later acquired by Platinum Technology, Inc.)

The problem with wide acceptance of knowledge-based systems continues to be standards. Knowledge-based system are not interoperable alternatives, but proprietary adventures. Unlike other enabling technologies, such as C++ or SQL, each knowledge-based tool vendor maintains a proprietary syntax and semantics. Only at the most conceptual level do skills translate from one product to another. From the way objects are located to the syntax of rules, nothing is the same.

Of course, like extensions to SQL, the vendors claim superiority from their diversity. The right tool for the right job. But as other data processing contingencies have discovered, it is better to differentiate within a common framework. A couple of years ago the Carnegie Group, Digital Equipment Corporation, Ford Motor Company,

Texas Instruments, and US West started the Initiative for Managing Knowledge Assets (IMKA). They took the core representations of Carnegie's KnowledgeCraft and recreated them in elegant C++ libraries. Only a few vendors recognized the IMKA standard. TI no longer sells AI tools.

IMKA, however, was a move in the right direction. Proprietary Cs, FORTRANs, COBOLs, and BASICs share common roots from vendor to vendor. A basic level of understanding translates across implementations. The knowledge-based systems community needs to realize their common conceptual roots and work toward synergy.

The needed synergy is not likely. New players will emerge that combine the world of objects with the world of knowledge. The captive world of the inference engine transform into more sociable objects. Already major hardware vendors, like HP, are exploring new ways of implementing knowledge. The future of knowledge-based systems will not contain isolated islands of knowledge, but knowledge fully integrated with enterprise computing resources.

An Objective Future

The world of objects and the world of knowledge-bases will converge in a new object-oriented paradigm. Intelligent objects, called agents, will roam the networks inside and outside of corporations. Agents will negotiate, cooperate, and fight within cyberspace. The inference engine will remain, but the focus will be on tight beams of knowledge, encapsulated in agent.

The commercial world of inference engines populated by objects will contract in favor of intelligent objects that work within and across products like Microsoft Word or Microsoft Excel or Lotus cc:Mail. Rather than going to large knowledge-bases looking for answers, small knowledge bases will cooperate to answer questions. Agents will help suggest phrases, help develop equations, or answer mundane e-mail.

Putting knowledge into the system will remain a problem, but the problem will take advantage of all the object knowledge that came before. The world's largest knowledge-based system, MCC's CYC, uses objects to represent its views of the world. The common sense in CYC will become the foundation for more specialized knowledge entities. Rather than capture domain specific knowledge and commonsense knowledge associated with it, future knowledge engineers will concentrate on domain knowledge within an established framework. AI and objects will create a unique electronic community.

While at MCC working on the Orion project, Won Kim envisioned that object-oriented databases would one day reason. Tools like case-based reasoning and intelligent search routines are already finding themselves in the specifications and beta versions of the next-generation databases. The next logical step in the evolution of computing will be the synthesis of objects and reason. We have simplified programming down to minute elements of code and data. It is time that the code and data learn how to behave in the greater computing community.

Their value is in current tools. Their ability to rapidly develop applications in the client/server environment has breathed new life into the unfocused AI industry. If you need to develop distributed GUI- object-oriented systems, commercial knowledge-based tools will likely save money and time. The risk comes from using today's tools to build tomorrow's legacy systems. Each project must weigh the short-term advantage of quick-gratification, leading-edge technology with the interoperable, scaleable, and standards-based future.

METHODS TO THE MADNESS

When I was a second grade student, I started to learn about methods. How to count, how to read, how to spell. the methods contained rules that continue to influence me as I check this manuscript for spelling and punctuation. If you are reading this, we share a method of communication. We take the common semantics and syntax of English for granted. The computer industry continues to search for a means of manipulating symbols that does so with the elegance and simplicity of human language.

When you talk about methods for object-oriented systems, the discussion can be exhausting. When you add other technologies to the discussion, it becomes mind boggling. But in our heterogeneous reality, with its character-based history and intelligent agent future, it has become necessary to grapple with our lack of methods. Yes, lack of methods. If you take any single technology view, be it relational databases and terminals or a pure object approach, the complexity of the debate narrows to a few contending methods, which differ more in style than in final result. But mix technologies, and the world of methods ceases to exist.

Visualize an object-oriented GUI to be built in Smalltalk. This GUI is the entry point to a relational database, a legacy IMS database, and an expert system. I can model the GUI in Rumbaugh, Booch, or Martin/Odell. I model the databases using Chen with an information engineering flare. The expert system derives from Bechtel Software's KADS OBJECT. I cannot show, in one place, the dynamic query generated to the relational database by the expert system that triggers an IMS lookup from a piece of procedural code written in Smalltalk. I cannot show a direct mapping between database fields and the object fields in the GUI. In the plethora of methods, no method exists to model my system. For large corporations migrating from mainframe COBOL and networked databases to distributed client/server computing implemented in relational databases and objects, the lack of tools and methods is a problem in and of itself.

Understanding AI Methods

Before we attempt a solution to the method interaction problem, I should familiarize you with the basic methods used by the AI community. If you ask a researcher at a university or a practitioner in a corporation, they may not have a name for what they do. In fact, they may claim no method to their development process. Unlike C, Pascal, and COBOL jockeys, AI hacks never really adopted a structured programming gospel. In the AI community, the brain was too messy to be captured in stringent, sterile phrases parsed identically time after time.

That would be true if the AI community was actually capturing the brain, but it isn't. Except in the rarest of research projects, AI only mimics learned activity, most of which is learned from stringent and sterile textbooks. Of course, the value of AI is that it also captures experiential knowledge—knowledge learned on the job, not from a textbook. The main difference, however, between experiential knowledge and textbook knowledge is the fact that no one has yet bothered to write it down.

Unlike traditional programming, where the world comes packaged neatly into algorithms, AI programs don't come neatly at all. Even the worst of tax laws remains interpretable by a trained accounting

programmer and her customers. Each calculation and its relationship
to previous results is spelled out in excruciating detail.

Not so with human intelligence. Not only do we fail to communicate neatly, we also fail to store our knowledge neatly. The best
expert systems contain knowledge extracted after weeks and
months of prying, prodding, and poking. Because AI practitioners
often adhere to the rapid prototyping school, much of their code
splashes onto a monitor within hours or days after an interview.
Rather than showing a design, AI programmers show results. Their
fantastic tools for displaying frame hierarchies and rule interactions
preclude the use of structured techniques.

Or so they think. One reason AI remains a closet discipline is its
inability to repeat itself with rapidity and accuracy. For some problems, the human mind is as prosaic as a tax tome. For AI systems
wishing to capture expertise, methods can be applied.

The most widely known AI methods is KADS (Knowledge Acquisition and Structuring) developed by ESPRIT (European Strategic Pro-
gramme for Research and Development in Information Technology).
Bechtel Software, Inc., in San Francisco, refined KADS into KADS
OBJECT, and Bolesian Systems of Helmond, The Netherlands, used
KADS as the basis for their SKE (Structured Knowledge Engineering)
methodology.

KADS describes a model-driven approach to knowledge acquisition and development. In Bechtel's KADS OBJECT, the following four
models combine to represent the logical view of an AI system's
knowledge and its structure. (See Table 2.2 for a comparison of traditional AI, and its emphasis on prototyping, with the more structured approach of KADS OBJECT.)

    ☑ The KADS OBJECT DOMAIN MODEL captures concepts
       about a domain of knowledge, the attributes of these con-
       cepts, and their relationships to each other. Eventually the
       concepts become classes.

    ☑ The INFERENCE MODEL documents the inferencing mecha-
       nism that reasons best about a given set of concepts. The
       inference model's problem-solving templates may include
       diagnosis, scheduling, monitoring, classification, and so forth.

    ☑ In the TASK MODEL, KADS captures the detailed tasks per-
       formed by the expert. A variety of interview and observation

techniques are used to see how an expert actually performs his or her task. An associated inference model describes the reasoning used to accomplish each task.

☑ Finally, the STRATEGIC MODEL details the sequencing of tasks, what knowledge is required when, and how information is passed from task to task.

The four logical models interact in a knowledge matrix that illustrates the relationships between tasks, inference models, strategic knowledge, and domain knowledge. The physical design translates the knowledge matrix into the classes, objects, and behaviors that will execute the model.

Table 2.2: Comparing Rapid Prototyping with KADS OBJECT

Rapid Prototyping	*KADS OBJECT*
data driven	model driven
no guidance in knowledge acquisition	guidance in knowledge acquisition
prototyping as an approach	prototyping as a tool
direct from expert to code	phased approach
hard to control and plan	easier to control and plan
uncertainty about end result	greater certainty about end result
no intermediate deliverables	intermediate deliverables
hard to maintain; opaque	easier to maintain; transparent
no audit trail	emphasis on design traceability
poor design documentation	excellent design documentation

Source: Bechtel Software, Inc.

KADS was not designed to solve the problem of thinking machines. It was developed to provide structure to certain tasks that have proven amenable over and over to computer-based reasoning.

There was no attempt in KADS to describe computer reasoning in esoteric terms. KADS was an attempt to make knowledge engineering repeatable for a given class of problems. Most knowledge-based systems today fit into one of its inference models and use objects/frames to represent the people, concepts, and things in a system.

Despite its valiant attempt, KADS doesn't go far enough. Knowledge-based systems developed in objects and rules don't cover the gamut of possible solutions. As of this writing, no widespread formal methods exist for employing genetic algorithms, abduction systems, distributed AI, neural networks, or case-based reasoning. For now, though, we will proceed with what we have.

Technology Interaction Diagrams

Although the AI community is developing methods, the existence of expert-system development methods does nothing to solve our interaction dilemma. Most of the expert systems that exist do so outside the traditional development cycle. Most of them do not rely on the management information sciences department and some run on unfriendly hardware, like LISP workstations.

The objects in a KADS OBJECT model are not necessarily first class objects when viewed from a C++ or Visual Basic program. In fact, the interaction between a C++ application and the expert system may itself require a great amount of time and skill.

In an attempt to integrate these models, I developed the idea of technology interaction diagrams (TIDs). I will discuss object diagrams generically, since I believe any object diagramming techniques could encompass TIDs.

Objects form the core of TIDs. No data types exist that cannot be encapsulated, accessed, and manipulated within objects. Some of the new data types that TIDs would encapsulate include legacy mainframe applications, expert systems, relational databases, and other external systems, both automated and non-automated.

Expertise captured within an object system is not modeled as external. A TID does nothing to facilitate the integration of state-transition diagrams, for instance, and object task models. That is a subject for another day.

Unlike pure object hierarchies, which decompose from object class to object instance, instances in TIDs can decompose into other technologies. A relational database class would contain the methods for interacting with a relational database. The relational database itself would simply be data to be acted upon within the object model. At the high level, the object model remains one of object classification and collaboration. At lower levels, a wide variety of models may exist, including network databases, hierarchical databases, legacy COBOL applications, and others.

A new technology that adds complexity is workflow. Workflow automates the movement of information within an enterprise. Most workflow systems today exist as separate applications that indirectly interact with desktop and network applications. Future workflow systems are likely to evolve into either network services, or like examples I provided in "AI and Objects" in *Object Magazine* (Rasmus, Daniel W., "AI and Objects," *Object Magazine*, May/June 1993), as services within the enterprise object structure.

Many of the ideas behind workflow are similar to those in AI. Workflow models capture expertise in rules and manage objects of information. The expertise captured in workflow is primarily procedural, so it attacks only the low end of the AI spectrum. Unlike AI, which is a general-purpose technology, workflow is a vertical technology focused on the movement and management of work.

In terms of TIDs, workflow and AI can be treated as both underlying technologies and integrated behaviors. If the expert system or workflow system already exists, it would make sense to communicate with it using its application programming interface. If they do not exist, it might make sense to tightly couple to workflow and intelligence aspects of new systems within the object behaviors. Workflow and AI are simply alternatives to implementing processes within an application.

TIDs can help bridge the technology gap, allowing established paradigms that include other technologies to decompose into lower-level abstractions. It maintains the integrity of object models by encapsulating all the foreign code—and because it encapsulates it, the method remains able to absorb new technologies as they evolve.

Making the CASE

Artificial intelligence remains underutilized. Unfulfilled expectations account for much of this, but more stems from nonstandard implementations of those areas in which AI has been successful. Rule-based systems and inference engines are clearly mature and useful. Thousands of documented systems exist. If you work in a small company, though, chances are you've never seen one.

AI has always been outside: special hardware, special languages, and special methods. The methods will remain the same, but it is clear that C or Smalltalk can easily create robust inference engines, complete with rules and frames. Most of today's AI applications already run on workstations, PCs, and Macs. Objects enable our artificial intelligence to flourish in cyberspace. Already intelligent agents, like those in MIT's actor model, are acting independently to weave connections between human and machine. Standard methods and standard syntax will allow us to leverage the potential of our intelligent microcode creations.

It is time for the methodologists to consider the big picture. No single software technique will suffice for the '90s, let alone 2000 and beyond. Multimedia will require intelligent navigation. The shrinking work force will require fewer people to make more decisions. Some level of intelligent system will be required to assist them. The complexity of our infrastructure will require automated design and monitoring. The huge vistas of information that pour forth from the human mind will remain underapplied without tools for maneuvering through them.

Today we continue to seek the elusive mimicry of our brain. That is fine and good. The intellectual challenge of copying ourselves will generate new knowledge about how we think. But that adventure has already generated much that is useful. It is for those of us practicing information engineering to employ AI techniques that have already found their way into our bags of tricks. We should not do this spuriously, however. The structured techniques that we preach should apply to all of our software manufacturing. A new technique should not preclude us from designing our product. Even if we use every technique available to us, we will be judged not so much by our innovation today as by our handiwork's ability to adapt to future requirements.

If we continue to build applications without thought, we will create a new generation of legacy applications—and the debate about how we do it right will belong not to us, but the next generation of second graders to which the computer is an integral part of their learning experience. For them, the methods we struggle to evolve and adopt will fit together as seamlessly as English prattle between two stockbrokers.

TESTING THE LOGIC

I once spent almost an entire day coaching a networking outsourcer on the importance of testing a firewall. "If you can't test it, then I'm not sure I believe it's secure," I said over and over. The lack of processes for identifying alerts or updating software were less important than a rigorous test that would identify flaws implemented elsewhere in the tenuous set of tools that acts as a moat between my company and the wild world of the Net. But as I made these demands I kept thinking about how I used to test expert systems, or not. It was nearly impossible to figure out what kind of input to plan for. Expert systems are such fragile slices of knowledge that an unplanned input of even the slightest deviation could send an inferencing session off into Sillyville.

I remember the classic case of a rusty Volkswagen described to a medical expert system. As the system gathered external data, such as color, blotchy red areas, and an above normal temperature, it was clear the expert system was not going to ask anything that would differentiate between a car and a human being. In the end, we discovered, much to the dismay of the mechanic, that the Volkswagen had contracted measles.

Expert systems and firewalls share a common trait. It is less likely, over time, that what the system was designed to detect and control will change. Knowledge evolves. Subtle shifts, meaningless over the course of a day or week, add up to very significant changes in world views that invalidate a system's underlying assumptions. In fact, in a recursive twist so common to AI, it is necessary to test the test. A test itself is based on the same fundamental assumptions as the system. As knowledge evolves, the tests will become obsolete. In the firewalls, it might be new IP spoofing techniques or massive programs aimed at several iterations of attack within a few seconds.

Computer virus testers are perhaps the most aware of this phenomenon. Their tests, at any given time, can only test for known viruses. I remember purchasing version 3.0 of a popular virus protection program. The literature touted it as "adaptive." Download a new profile and the virus checker would contain search and eradication data for the latest digital virus. Well, my machine is now equipped with version 4.5 because clever hackers invented entirely new types of viral attacks that the adaptive program could not adapt to. The hackers changed the rules of the game, which forced the digital clinicians to rethink their strategies.

Testing in an evolving field is not impossible. The temporal aspects of test are important, though. A test is only good at a certain time, and then it ages into uselessness. And the results of that test may be good for even less time. But testing should not be ignored; it should just become a well-considered member of planning and execution, not put off until the last minute before rolling out a system. Testing is about knowledge and knowledge requires constant vigilance.

Testing Intelligent Systems

It has often been suggested that test plans should precede design, because that way a design will include all the features being tested. The goal of the system is to pass the test, which helps focus development and avoid dead ends of design.

I have really never employed this technique. I guess, though, that I consider a system specification a bit like a test plan. A good system specification, when written precisely, reflects the end state functionality of a system. A test plan on the system is just a semantic reorientation that restates a functional assertion as a goal. The test plan should, however, include several levels of detail that test for conditions in the actual implementation of a feature, not simply for the feature's existence.

Some of the test items in intelligent systems are the same as those of traditional systems. Are correct values written to a database? Does the logic fire in the correct sequence, producing meaningful results? Is the user interface properly coupled to the logic so an appropriate window gathers the expected data? If I turn on a trace, does the logic leading to a particular conclusion make sense?

The difference comes with the logic, and can be very complicated when dealing with object systems that invoke methods. The given state of the system will trigger an event. The large intelligent systems defy a confidence that all states are accounted for. Unlike payroll system designers, knowledge engineers usually include a disclaimer about 100 percent accuracy. "We tested for what we knew," we tell out customers, "but if the world changes, or the expert remembers something they failed to tell us, or the expert learns something new, you may invalidate portions of this system."

A few rules of thumb, nonetheless, help eliminate chance error in programming, leveling the risk as the knowledge content itself, rather than poor programming technique. Here are a few good heuristics for examining intelligent system code:

- ☑ Check for duplicate rules that contain conflicting results.

- ☑ Verify that if the same result can come from multiple rules, those rules are both necessary and reflect real conditions.

- ☑ Check all outputs in the design, and verify that a rule exists to generate that output.

- ☑ Look for rules that generate outputs that are not specified in the design.

- ☑ Make sure any procedural code releases control to the inference engine and does not interfere with the natural firing of rules.

- ☑ Double-check spelling in all conditions, especially those that chain to other rules.

- ☑ During a runtime test, make sure that all of the input requests are expected. An unexpected input request may mean that a rule to derive that input is improbably phased, missing, or contains a misspelled object.

You check for mistakes, but on a big system with much interaction, it is often difficult to test everything. As my readers know, I am big on categorization. Taking system and unit testing into account when modularizing a system enhances the test experience. It also makes it easier to extract bits of knowledge when they are no longer contributory to the current knowledge base.

Designing for Test

When I worked at Western Digital, I was involved with design for test projects. We designed printed circuit boards with easily accessible test points, making it easy to test the board. We even designed circuits into chips that allowed the logic on the board to report anomalies during manufacturing.

About this same time, I wrote a complete GUI system builder for Nexpert Object. It started with nothing but a blank HyperCard and then fired off the inference session. As the questions were presented, the HyperCard stack generated the GUI on the fly, based on the question being presented and its data type. It even suspended the inference so I could arrange a card and place graphics. By building the GUI during execution, I could test for sequence and ensure that all data was properly accounted for, since the GUI was built directly from the contents of the knowledge base.

As I found during the development of this HyperCard GUI system, designing for test involves understanding logic groupings, refraining, whenever possible, from rules and control structures that act at a universal level. Even if the data element exists across rule groups, the instantiation of values should be tightly controlled so that the sequence of events leading to a given state are clearly understood. In other words, don't let the system decide when it needs a universal variable; force them into a logical flow that appears intuitive to the end user.

While building GUIs with the tool, I discovered many of my own programming faults. My horrible spelling resulted in dead ends that required more than one rule be corrected before the inferencing could proceed. I now find using a data dictionary invaluable. Find the object or method in the data dictionary and insert it at the appropriate place. I only need to spell the name correctly once that way. I don't know how I ever managed to write code by hand. Perhaps my laziness for details was a key factor in my choice of higher-level languages over code that required me to manage pointers and garbage collection.

Finally, design with the end result in mind. Programmers too often get trapped with the elegance of code and forget that the important result is not some hidden feature, but the external output of the system. If the system is designed with the functional results as the overarching concern, they will be more testable than one focused on internal technical elegance.

Testing My Conclusions

It is hard to test intelligent systems. Creating the test plan and executing the tests brings both programmer and customer face to face with the fragility of their knowledge and point, even as it is fresh and new, to its eventual demise into obsolescence. All computer systems, though, add value for only short periods of time. We should see this neither as a disadvantage nor an excuse for not testing. As I told my firewall crew today, I don't want to hear that some common technique was used to breach the corporate firewall. If that happens, there will be hell to pay. If something new and unforeseen attacks and succeeds, it will be just another opportunity to learn.

LEGACY KNOWLEDGE-BASED SYSTEMS

When I hear the word legacy, I think mainframe and COBOL, IMS and dBase III. Knowledge-based systems, if you examine them in the light of standards and technology evolution, begin to look as much like legacy applications as a CICS application running in a Windows 95 terminal emulator. Their rules fit no standards and many interfaces appear arcane.

Several years ago, expert-system suppliers touted their product as the next generation tool of choice. Smart applications, it seemed, were poised to take over the world. It didn't happen—at least not yet. The primary reason for the lack of AI's infiltration into the mainstream of development came from a lack of interoperability; a long, mysterious development cycle; and very dynamic knowledge domains.

Many expert systems were developed in places where their expertise was built more around process than a developing field of knowledge. As the company changed, the expertise in the system required maintenance. A good example is a help desk. An expert system built around Microsoft Office 3.0 does little to help a caller with a Microsoft Word 6.0 problem, which requires Microsoft Office 4.2 expertise.

But it is not just the expertise in artificial intelligence systems that qualifies them for legacy equal to an RPG-based accounts payable system. The technology within expert-system products is starting to show its age. Some tools rely on interpreted languages, and those languages have continued to grow. It is rare, however, to find tools built on LISP or Prolog. Most knowledge-based tools found their way to C and SQL and there they stayed. They know how to talk to relational databases and they are probably client/server. Some expert systems, however, remain even more legacy than that.

Code for expert systems still remains on mainframes. Many traditional expert-system products do not fit into the new architectures of

Java, Intranets, or distributed computing. That can be said of many other classes of software as well, but it is especially disconcerting given the renewed shift toward software that contains knowledge or acts intelligent. New classes of software, such as agents, often arrive from entrepreneurial sources rather than traditional AI companies. Over recent years many expert-system companies have reinvented their image, if not their products. As they move back toward their core technology to leverage trends in agents or reengineering or knowledge management, they find new competitors and eroded mind share. They also find whole new technologies, like groupware, competing for once-strategic markets.

As we head toward the year 2000, all of the new technologies will come to bear, even on the most mundane of applications. I cannot imagine that SAP and PeopleSoft will not take the tools of modern computing and converge them as they have enterprise data models. Wizards will help configure applications and guide users. Agents will exchange data and collaborate on tough problems, while genetic algorithms will find near optimal solutions to problems with large search spaces. The technology will be focused on smaller chunks in knowledge more easily maintained because it will be knowledge invented for automation rather than automated knowledge. As Microsoft can attest, it is easier to write a Chart Wizard and guide a novice than it is to use expertise from the masses to chart the future.

Expert systems, however, have many legacies. As with all technology, we can write bridges or build custom interfaces. Technology will evolve, but the other legacies of environment, expertise, and focus haunt the knowledge components of AI systems, making their histories and their futures expensive to maintain.

Legacy Knowledge

Knowledge presents another problem. There is no way around legacy knowledge. It is not enough to simply decide to eliminate the knowledge, toss it away, and restart. That knowledge may still have value to the enterprise. So instead of removing the knowledge from service, it might be better placing it into a knowledge repository on the Web, entered into a corporate knowledge management program with appropriate metadata so it can be found by curious corporate historians and others seeking to leverage an organization's expertise.

Even if you don't have a knowledge management scheme yet, knowledge management is the key to eliminating legacy knowledge. Let's back up a few steps, perhaps a few years first.

Most AI systems were built by departments for focusing on tasks, but often tasks of grand scale and deep intellectual challenge. They rely heavily on individual experts or teams of experts. Good AI applications were personal quests and private triumphs. These expert systems may not have even survived, and if they did, their survival itself relied on perseverance by lone contributors. Rarely did a corporation, at its highest levels, recognize an expert system as the "thing to invest in" once it was completed.

With the advent of knowledge management, corporations increasingly recognize the value of knowledge. They fight for top technical and marketing talent. They closely guard intellectual capital like patents, inventions, and copyrights. And in the broad scope of knowledge management, expertise stored in computer systems becomes part and parcel of the *stuff* with which chief knowledge officers concern themselves.

Knowledge management attempts to build an ongoing appreciation for knowledge and to put into place processes for sharing knowledge and maintaining its value. Anecdotes bubble up incessantly about the desk of the retired engineer and its myriad cryptic notes stuck in drawers. The expertise of a lifetime condensed into several dozen pieces of paper about designing airplane wings or avoiding metal corrosion in salt water.

Legacy expert systems happen because the knowledge was not the challenge in the long run. The original expert system, despite the marketing hype of its business case, performed only as expected until something in the business changed: product, environment, or personnel. I have watched expert systems deteriorate as one expert ascends the corporate latter over the expert who developed the system. Typical expert systems do not reflect *the* way, but *a* good way of doing something. If an expert with *a* different way comes into political power, the expertise of the system becomes as discounted as the human expert passed over for promotion.

In the case of products and buildings, those too may affect the expert system. Many manufacturing systems were built with particular machines and configurations in mind. Change out a machine and its time to update the expert system with new parameters. The new machine may be able to do things not conceived of by the original development team. Even a GUI for adding new equipment fails to properly represent the new equipment. Basic rules, algorithms, interface routines, and other elements may change. In legal systems, laws and regulations shift and modify, making any expertise based on them challenged to retain currency.

Product shifts also move knowledge toward obsolescence. I once worked for a computer product manufacturing company that went from being the world's largest supplier of Winchester disk drive controllers to being an everything-to-everybody computer products supplier to a major manufacturer of hard disks. Expert systems written for divested or discontinued product lines meant little. Sometimes the expertise could be transferred, but it was easier to use the same people than to rewrite a system that took two and a half years to develop. People, it seemed, were more adaptable.

Avoiding a Legacy

In the old days, a legacy was a good thing. Legacies were handed down from the past, but mostly in a positive sense. Legacy systems certainly are handed down, but unlike a castle or a reputation for heroism, a legacy mainframe or Novell system often finds the recipient less than joyous upon confirmation of the bequest.

It is from the field of artificial intelligence and its intersection with genetic algorithms, chaos theory, and complexity studies that finds the answer to legacy knowledge. We need to start building software capable of adapting to its environment—perhaps in the beginning—in small ways, such as suggesting how to map fields from a recently integrated Oracle database or by sending up alerts when interfaces appear expanded or changed.

Human knowledge, we are finding, comes from small bits of knowledge converging on an answer rather than large parcels of expertise concentrated into large knowledge constructs with well-defined edges. Cooperating agents with problem solving skills, perceptions, and knowledge-encoding routines will eventually prove much more flexible in capturing and maintaining knowledge than expert systems did with their hand-crafted expertise.

Objects afford us the ability to create small applications that can look for change and report it back. They provide the core technology for applications code that can integrate, but act independently. Monolithic COBOL running payroll cannot examine itself or its environment. In an OO application pieces can be concerned with the present task, others with the environment, and still others with planning the future. These disparate activities can coalesce into meaningful behavior much like cells cooperate to form living things. At one point our cells were individual creatures that found advantages to working together. We can design software with much the same thoughts in mind.

And as with natural selection, the pace need not be rapid, nor the conclusions immediate. Software will be around for a long time. We can start building code that does a task, and then add something to it without really changing its function, placing new methods or objects for contingency purposes. Sometimes we will find that objects designed for one thing, with small modifications, may be used for something else. And when we find software adapting to new laws, new products, and new people with little human intervention, how then will we classify these new adaptive systems? And what legacies will they leave behind?

3

THE OO-AI
RELATIONSHIP

OK, so you read all of the preliminary stuff and are now ready for the meat of this book. This is the "techie" chapter, if indeed I have a "techie" chapter. Here I discuss rules and client/server architectures, object-oriented databases, and IS management. And after you're done reading it, I hope the experiences conveyed in these AI anecdotes help you understand why OO needs AI.

WHY OO NEEDS AI

It is quite logical that object-oriented programming needs artificial intelligence; at least if you examine current business trends, the logic will appear impeccable. Over the past couple of years phrases like "knowledge management" and "business rules" have emerged with much the same business intent as they had during AI's heyday. But they have emerged with different technology, or at least with the intelligence conveyed less the artificial part. Today phrases like "knowledge management," "workflow," and "business rules" mean a myriad of things, ranging from groupware to databases to intellectual capital management. The goal remains to structure, capture, hone, communicate, and harness knowledge.

If AI did nothing else, its failures pointed out the dramatic messiness of knowledge. During the late '80s and early '90s software evolved to deal with our messy interactions. E-mail skyrocketed and groupware slowly became an acceptable means, if not a strategic necessity, for sharing unstructured information. The Web exploded with the theme of "content is king." Knowledge, especially digitally encoded knowledge, pushed into nearly every large corporation, many smaller businesses, and even into the home office.

And along with the reemergence of knowledge as a strategic element of business, object-oriented programming went from novelty to universal client in the form of Java. No one doubts objects anymore. Java became widely accepted almost immediately. It was clear that objects held the key to distributed, heterogeneous application development. Not only did the Web bring content to the forefront, for the first time in decades, the Web offered a chance to define a truly universal client. Java and Web browsers ran on everything: Windows 95, NT, UNIX, Macintosh, and even OS/2.

And as those phrases about knowledge and content began to weave their way into popular programming jargon, the need for technologies to support them emerged. In many cases, agents played an important role in defining groupware search, Web-based shopping, and workflow routines. Agents provided the metaphor for releasing one's surrogate into cyberspace.

AI provided the framework for objects on the Internet. The distribution of individuals, their collaboration on problem solving, and their negotiating skills come from AI. Although objects will act as the underlying representational structure, the ideas about how objects interact come from AI. Without AI's anthropomorphic tendencies, and the tenacity to describe distribution mechanisms with real-world applications, objects might not have been prepared for the potential of the 'Net.

AI also helps frame many other problems related to objects, from proper ways to structure object hierarchies to the control of the execution of methods.

AI also contributed to the high-level use of interpreted programming. Many of us experienced programming for the first time through the ROMs of early Apple and Radio Shack computers. Interpretation within objects creates the possibility of learning. Dynamic creation of classes and other structures allow applications to adapt to new challenges not originally conceived by their programmers. As integrated systems become more sophisticated, adaptable code will remove the fragility that plagues both AI and conventional systems. When applications encounter large changes, such as modified business rules, or minor changes, like redefined data, they cease to function. They are programmed only for the known and contain no code for contingent events. In nature, the code of DNA presents so many possibilities that species find ways over time to modify their very architecture in order to cope with the stress of environmental changes and competition.

But in applications and machines, we engineer the contingency out of the system. We idealize the code so that it runs tersely through processors, knowing that a programmer will always be there to fix it should it break.

Perhaps another perspective could inform this practice. Perhaps we leave access to unused libraries open, perhaps we give applications access to their own internals, allowing them to try different bits now and then to help overcome some deficiency in their impeccable routines. The very imperfections in DNA allow it to change itself and, ultimately, organisms.

Object-oriented applications are excellent structures for supporting adaptation in software. They are modular and can support the exchange of relatively small portions of their structure without damaging the overall functionality of the application. An OO application could easily gain additional object types, incorporating additional logic, even intuition, as they exchange and merge their resources with the resources of the agents.

Adaptability may seem a distant concept, but it is a necessary one given the rising complexity of application. Some systems already approach a level of complexity that overwhelms any one human's ability to understand it beyond a few levels of abstraction. Like the old story of the blind men and the elephant. Each touches it and thinks he feels some other kind of animal. With large complex applications, programmers often work on fragments of applications for which they have little understanding of its impact, interactions, or integration. Adaptable applications may be the only way to keep complex, integrated applications synchronized with ever changing business rules.

It is not just innovative architectures and the merging of digital and natural worlds that bring AI and object together. AI techniques add a new dimension to even the most common applications. Adobe's PageMaker 6.5 incorporates object-oriented AI to help designers and artists maintain page layouts when they switch output devices. Manufacturing systems use objects and AI to better refine material requirements and schedule work in factories. AI assesses loans and helps process insurance claims more swiftly.

Objects form the structure; they contain the procedural code and handle user interfaces. But as applications require heightened abilities to understand their data, to adapt to changing situations, to make decisions from myriad inputs, AI will provide the context for those programming discussions. AI techniques will transform simple applications into sophisticated assemblages that assist humans by pointing out discrepancies and errors that might elude us through the numbness of repetition.

This chapter outlines several ideas intended to help OO programmers see the benefits of including AI concepts in their day-to-day coding repertoire. AI helps consider difficult issues like how persistent objects work and how they represent memory—either application, human, or organizational. AI, of course, introduces rules, reasoning, and neural networks. Each of these techniques expands a programmer's skills, allowing them to create applications that extend the boundaries of conventional code. In their most sophisticated interactions, AI and Objects blend so that the reasoning seems an integral part of the overall application. End users need not know they employ AI, they need to see only the simplicity of interaction as an application answers a question, modifies a layout, or presents its case for a home loan to a young couple.

We praise our intelligence as the characteristic that sets us apart from other creatures. As Henri Bergson said, "Intelligence ... is the faculty of making artificial objects, especially tools to make tools." Software represents perhaps our most powerful tool, because it, unlike forklifts and jackhammers, increases our mental acuity rather than our physical strength. We can do no more honor to our species than to attempt to capture some fragment of its essence in benefit of the future. Objects need AI not simply to expand their possibilities, but to provide a connection between us and ourselves. AI provides the only means known at this time to imbue our software creations with the ability to build upon themselves, for tools to make tools.

LEARNING HOW TO KNOW

Much of the material in chapters 1 and 2 concentrated on technology. AI technology, however, acts only as a repository for knowledge. Knowing how to turn the ramblings of a high-strung expert into lines of C becomes more important than the tool used to represent the rules. This section will introduce a few key elements of knowledge acquisition (KA), which was touched upon in Chapter 2, "Learning from Artificial Intelligence." Later sections will examine KA in more detail and investigate technologies that help gather knowledge from people and from non-human sources, like databases.

I will start with simple KA examples suitable for supporting help desk calls, analyzing a failed computer board, or classifying drilling sites. These are mostly heuristic tasks that require little more than rules reasoning over a set of objects for completion. Some AI problems require linear programming or genetic algorithms to add meat to their human heuristics. We will concentrate on rule-of-thumb knowledge and experience.

Find the Right Expert

Having a problem to solve is not enough. Knowing that a knowledge-based solution fits technology to problem is not enough. You need the expert—and I don't just mean physically. You need the expert as believer and advocate, willing experimenter, and reviewer. You need his or her, body and soul.

Finding people that exhibit this kind of trust is difficult, because building a knowledge-based system, while ego-gratifying, also threatens the very essence of the expert: his or her expertise. The purpose of an expert system is to distribute knowledge and retain knowledge. Knowledge distribution removes the expert from day-to-day need by making what they know immediately accessible to the organization. Knowledge retention means that even if the expert leaves, his or her expertise remains.

So you need to seek motivation. I found motivation for one expert system in the fact that the experts didn't want to do what they were experts at. In the case of Western Digital's Surface Mount Assembly Reasoning Tool (SMART), the experts were more interested in designing next generation manufacturing processes than writing programs to support the current manufacturing line. The experts willingly provided time and knowledge so they could concentrate on designing future manufacturing process.

The ideal situation is to have one expert. But because of egos or lack of breadth, it is often necessary to integrate multiple expert opinions. This may prove as much political maneuver as information systems skill. In the SMART system multiple experts participated, and in some cases disagreed. Knowledge engineers modeled multiple versions and allowed system performance to determine the correct path. Other systems may not lend themselves to such analysis.

Sometimes the disagreements call for an expert caucus where the experts can confront their differences. Like other aspects of knowledge acquisition, these confrontations and understandings often enhance process performance even before the first rule is written. They create a shared vision and often remove inefficiencies in manual processes that are carried forward and magnified by the expert system.

Organizations identify experts for you through not so subtle indications. If the expert can't find time to make an appointment, that is a good sign. The right expert is valued by the organization. For the knowledge acquisition to work, the organization must be willing to make the expert available to the project, often for tens or hundreds of hours. A good knowledge-based system requires commitment from the organization, the expert, and the information technology people involved in the project. Failure to commit at any point threatens the accuracy, schedule, and performance of the system.

Finding a good expert is difficult enough. Once you have one or two or ten you need to maximize your time with them. Failure to effectively elicit knowledge may require reworking to fill knowledge-base gaps, dragging out the schedule, annoying sponsors, and perhaps turning a cooperative expert into a grumpy expert.

The Interview

So you find a person who meets all the criteria. A serious organization with serious competitive pressures will find the right person. Now that you have that person, what do you do?

Because our most natural means of transferring information is speech, the interview has become the most popular form of knowledge acquisition. Many of the other techniques, like protocol analysis, repertory grids, and role playing, place people in unfamiliar circumstances, perhaps doing unfamiliar things, like interacting with software or performing for an audience.

The best interviews take place in comfortable surroundings where the expert can relax. It is best to remove the expert from the distractions of the workplace. Sometimes, however, holding one or two interviews in the expert's office can add new knowledge and give the knowledge engineer a sense for the environment in which the system will work. The expert's office provides context for discussion. A Post-It note stuck on a terminal, or a handy file, often augment the interview. The things in the room provide familiar discussion points for the expert, and the surroundings relax him or her into more normal speech patterns, opening up conversation to richer detail.

Knowledge engineers need to enter the knowledge acquisition session with a good toolbox. This toolbox should include a tape recorder and a note pad, including a pencil with plenty of refills. In addition, depending on the kind of knowledge being gathered, you may want large paper and an easel so the expert can draw, a video camera to capture instructive procedure recreations, and whatever props and equipment the expert needs to teach that day's lessons. Always test the equipment before each interview. Don't aggravate an expensive guru over dead batteries in a tape recorder.

Once the interview begins, let the expert act as teacher. Let him or her describe their process with few questions. Allow them to wander down rivulets of thought. Hold all the questions until after the expert has completed their mental journey. The seemingly laborious wandering may indeed be the process the expert uses for solving the problem. Simple questions at the wrong time may change the expert's mode of thought and divert him or her from their natural reasoning path—and that path may prove the difference between adequate performance of a system and expert performance.

Early on it would be advantageous for the expert to introduce frequently used concepts and vocabulary. It doesn't hurt to read trade magazines and books about the subject. Knowledge engineers should not attempt to be experts, but they should be familiar enough with the material so they don't waste time asking what a word means.

As interviews continue, knowledge engineers take a more active interest in what the expert may or may not know. Based on background material, previous interviews, and other information, the questions should probe for complete answers. Start adding the more subtle tones and make the implied specific.

Knowledge engineers can assume no source of information is definitive (unless there is only one source). Explorations about a printed circuit board may have turned up expert technicians, shop floor procedures, case histories, and a customer manual. The knowledge engineer is responsible for reconciling all sources of information.

If multiple sources of knowledge exist, interviews should be used to ferret out discrepancies between sources. The knowledge engineer turns from passive sponge to challenging student. Experts with eager minds will learn from the experience. Less secure experts may need coddling from ego deflating holes in their personal knowledge base.

The process of conducting interviews, extracting, codifying, and teasing knowledge from an expert is much different than the basic requirements of gathering taught in business data processing courses. Knowledge adds scores of processes that would not be revealed in an ordinary Joint Application Development (JAD). Knowledge changes the focus of an application from supporting macro business process to modeling its most intimate details. The introduction of heuristic human knowledge into an application adds new challenges to the entire application development life cycle.

Defining Objects and Knowledge

Of course, in object-oriented programming, you need to define the objects. I often use a highlighter to pick objects from the interview and then transfer the highlighted words to three-by-five-inch cards for later concept sorting (or into an outliner/mind mapper like Inspiration from Inspiration Software in Portland, Oregon). Concept sorting categorizes concepts and other potential objects in such a way that a knowledge engineer or programmer can derive a first-level class structure. The *things*—concepts and potential objects—become subjects for later interviews where the knowledge engineer documents what they do and how they are reasoned about.

There is an important distinction in capturing how an expert reasons and what a thing does—and the distinction leads to multiple approaches to solving the same problem.

Interviews with experts lead to traditional IF ... THEN knowledge bases. Case studies and repair records point to case-based reasoning.

There is yet another possibility. If the *things* are things like gate arrays and memory chips, they have functions that can be entered into a model-based system. Instead of finding heuristics, the model of the board simulates behavior. An open at a test point will trace back along the circuitry, displaying the faulty component. The expertise becomes that of the board and its construction and logic, rather than the heuristics of the expert or the collective wisdom of those who repaired it in the past.

This gives us three knowledge-based approaches to the same problem. It is difficult to know which is best. The model-based approach seems most reliable, but it may prove too complex and difficult to maintain as new versions of boards increase the number of models. The expert approach gets to critical rules quickly, but the expert may not remain an expert in quick cycle-time products like printed circuit boards. The expert, however, is likely to know how to troubleshoot items that don't yet appear in the repair depot, making the system more robust than the case-based approach. As knowledge gathers, however, case-based reasoning may prove the most economical to maintain, generating new data and new rules directly from the repair databases with little fiddling from knowledge engineering.

It is important to determine the eventual knowledge representation and inference techniques early in a project (not necessarily the final deployment language). These three divergent approaches may yield equally accurate knowledge bases. The pursuit of knowledge in each, however, requires different skills from the knowledge engineer and different ways of gathering and representing the knowledge.

Never Ending Knowledge Acquisition

Knowledge acquisition never ends, unless the business process it supports becomes stagnant or disappears. If a knowledge-based system fails to change with the organization, it rapidly becomes obsolete. Organization changes, design changes, changes in the world, changes in assumptions about the world, and hundreds of other factors can make the knowledge in expert systems obsolete, or even wrong. Not all expert systems are as trivial as the printed circuit board example. Some, like the credit verification system at American Express, have evolved into mission critical applications. Inexact knowledge in these systems costs thousands or millions of dollars.

Inadequate knowledge about the stock market has made expert trading programs nose dive into endless sell cycles. Why? Because the existence of the expert trading programs changed the reality of the stock market. That new reality never found its way into expert trading system knowledge bases. None of them, I imagine, fired one rule that looked for the meteoric execution of buy and sell recommendations of its cousins. They just bought and sold, despite the existence of a rapid decline in the index. Unlike adaptive humans who can change assumptions on the fly, the knowledge-bases and neural networks of computer-based trading programs steadfastly actuate their goals based on assumptions, even when those assumptions are clearly incorrect to a knowledgeable human watching the melee.

There is more to coding expert systems than inference techniques and objects and frames. These systems generate subtle interactions between rules. As intelligent agents become more ubiquitous, the interactions will expand to the network, where message passing agents may erupt into cybernetic one-upsmanship.

Each rule—each demon—becomes an important system resource, requiring management and maintenance. The skills of the knowledge engineer are too finite to manage the complexity of an intelligent enterprise application. Enter the systems analyst of the future.

Systems Analysts for the Future

Working on business systems in the future will require a broader set of skills than those we find in people-titled systems analysts today. With a wide variety of technologies simultaneously maturing and converging, a systems analyst will need to be a constant student, polished team member, psychologist, knowledge engineer, business process modeler, and systems integrator. Those are big shoes to fill—and they will need to be filled.

The plethora of technologies like workflow, text retrieval, fourth-generation languages, object-oriented programming, ad hoc database access, and knowledge-based systems each add their own complexity to a discipline traditionally concerned with requirements definition, procedural languages, and reporting. Future analysts will work as support staff to systems that never stop evolving. In the new computing order, static lines of code become interpreted drag-and-drop realizations of end user whim and imagination. In the not too distant future, systems analysts will manage enhancements made by self-adapting systems as they hunt and peck their way through the Internet.

Because we use technology to gather, cut, and slice our databases, text, graphics, sound, and images, we need technology to help manage it. We need intelligent agents to tell us when something important enters cyberspace. We need knowledge of the business to build intelligent, object-oriented workflows that not only notify us of work we need to do, but proactively help us achieve our goals. And we need intelligent aids to assess the impact of changes on software, pinpointing that impact on other systems and monitoring self-adapting systems, while looking for signs of aberrant behavior or insight. Even with heightened skills, the systems analyst will need technology to help manage the technology.

Knowledge plays a key role in all of this—some of it simple, some of it complex, and most of it originating at one time or another from people. Objects will play a key role in encapsulating that knowledge and linking behavior to an object. Without a tight association of behavior and object we have no chance of managing the complex interactions that will take place along the Infobahn. Objects provide an essential chunking of knowledge and data required to let our minds relate to enormous volumes of information and ever more complex relationships systems.

Without the skills to acquire knowledge and integrate the right set of technologies, we have no chance at managing the onslaught of information we have requested. If we ask, it will come. Once the information arrives, we had better teach our systems what to do with it (and be prepared to act on the results). That will require people with the right skills to transform human intelligence into knowledge fragments ready to explore the nooks and grannies of cyberspace.

THE TOP TEN REASONS TO USE AI FOR CLIENT/SERVER

After his opening monologues David Letterman segues into his daily top ten list. So this seems like a good spot in this chapter to take a shot at my own top ten list: the top ten reasons to use AI for client/server.

10. Database Connectivity

Object-oriented expert system shells know how to access data in commercial relational databases. And many of them do it as well, if not better, than tools designed for the task. Once you use a database access product, you are pretty much stuck with tabular data, awaiting later massaging in a spreadsheet. Using an expert system shell, you can not only retrieve data, but store the results as dynamic objects and search for patterns, incongruities, and irregularities. Complex applications will take a lot of time and money, but a few simple rules to perform mundane analysis is, in some cases, less tedious than writing an Excel macro.

If you have complex structures to search (and who doesn't) the expert system can become an expert at building SQL queries. The expertise needed to build a good query is just as valuable as the expertise needed to the fix the exhaust system of a 1992 Chevy Cavalier. Build tools help users navigate the maze of data and select the right tables and attributes, and even suggest attributes based on other selections.

The combination of direct support for data access as well as rule-driven SQL development make expert systems formidable companions in the search for meaning in a sea of corporate data.

9.0 GUI Development Tools

AI invented GUIs. They do AI at the Palo Alto Research Center (PARC). What Steve Jobs saw on his infamous visit to PARC was a GUI influenced by AI environments. The connection between machine intelligence and intelligent ways of working is inseparable.

Kappa, Nexpert Object, Level Five Object, ADS, ART*Enterprise, and several others tools integrate the GUI with the inference engine. Logic becomes intelligent reactions to user events. A button click or prompt entry inspires a flurry of activity.

Even dedicated GUI development tools or new languages like Visual Basic will be hard pressed to match the eloquence and flexibility of expert system shell GUI tools.

8.0 Object-Oriented Programming

Objects? You were wondering when I would get to that. Previously I have discussed the differences between objects and frames. In client/server implementations, the differences mean little, much to the lament of Marvin Minsky and other proponents of frames. Frames and objects as they exist in tools encapsulate, send messages, inherit, abstract, and borrow from the past. And they add to number 7, high-level representations, as more understandable ways of describing computer programs. In short, expert system hybrid objects/frames provide the same benefits to programmers as their C++, Eiffel, or Smalltalk counterparts.

7.0 High-Level Representations

Getting a businessperson to understand even the best structured C is next to impossible. In fact, it should be impossible. The businessperson's job is not to understand code, it's to understand business. We MIS types want to be understood, so we invent things like CASE to help make our point. A data flow diagram, alas, still doesn't do much. With rules, however, experts can relate a little better. Just a little, mind you. Nothing we transform into program statements is going to totally bridge the gap between business and computing, but rules help.

With the high-level representations it is easy to say, "if these conditions are true, then we are going to move these objects over here." Or in better business English, "if we find purchase requisitions that haven't been filed and they were requested last week, we are going to put them into a list of late purchase requisitions and then trigger an e-mail message to the people who were supposed to do something about them." Each phrase of the sentence is tied directly to a rule clause. And then you turn to your customer and ask "will that work OK?" Objects add another degree of familiarity between analyst and programmer because the things in the environment remain classified and characterized like the things themselves, and not abstracted and broken into fragments.

High-level representations, of course, are not meant just for translation of computer programs into English for business people. They also make our jobs easier. By bumping the representations up a notch, we remove ourselves from the bits and bytes and begin thinking about manipulating objects with rules. *But you can't eke out the last drop of processor speed unless you write directly to the bus.* That statement probably rings true, but it misses the point—in most cases business systems no longer need to eke out the last drop of performance.

Performance today comes from high-speed networks, and fast workstations more than compensate for workarounds necessary in older Intel or Digital architectures. As for servers, nothing runs as fast as a terminal with a direct connection to the mainframe. Most users, though, willingly trade a few seconds of response time for increased integration, mice, and multimedia.

AI allows developers to concentrate on business logic rather than compiler peculiarities—and it brings the language of the computer a step closer to the language of the customer.

6.0 Cross-Platform Compatibility

Homogeneity seems a word close to extinction. Microsoft is working toward becoming the Big Blue for the '90s, but Apple and IBM refuse to allow total dominance. And the myriad UNIX suppliers make the computing market even more confusing. Several AI companies made the commitment to cross-platform support years before it was in vogue. Cross-platform compatibility sold software. Now it gives expert system companies a jump on tool suppliers.

5.0 Incremental Development

Perhaps the most important advantage of an OO expert system environment, and its biggest detraction, comes from the ability to build systems incrementally. Each object, each line of code adds to the system. A new rule can improve performance or it can make a once stable system behave like a refugee from Disneyland's Toontown.

Early delivery of results is a hallmark of AI development. It is so hard to explain AI stuff to people, but pretty easy to show them. Machine learning doesn't work well for complex business processes defined and changed by politics or whim. So people need to interface with an expert system to add new knowledge. An expert system is never completed, because like people, it must adapt to its changing environment and learn new facts, policies, or procedures. It can be difficult to cull business rules from traditional code. An expert system, with its much higher level of representations, makes incremental development more realistic. In this age of reengineering, it is important that our applications be as agile as their users and sponsors.

4.0 Embedability (APIs)

One of the problems with building everything inside an expert system shell is that you can't build everything inside an expert system shell.

Many decision-support applications are fine using nothing but objects and rules. Diagnostic systems and help desk systems may also work as self-contained systems. But if you want to automatically collect data from test equipment or pass messages across the network to another piece of software, you are likely going to call an external piece of code or wrap the entire expert system shell inside another application.

The nice thing about this is that AI companies have already realized this need. When developers realized stand-alone expert systems were not sufficient for solving real world problems, the AI companies started building libraries for embedding their logic engines inside traditional code. Some even went so far as to hide them under such prosaic tools as HyperCard and ToolBook.

You can still build your logic in the development environment and load it into the traditional C, FORTRAN, or Pascal code. You can still use database access. Some tools, like Nexpert Object, even let you run a client and observe rules and objects in the shell while the application executes. If you need to embed knowledge into a large application or add a few specialized functions to an expert system, hooking up to a shell extensibility is the only way to go.

3.0 True Clients

Client/server is still new. Market segments filled with host/terminal solutions look anemic to client/server shoppers. In manufacturing, for instance, material requirements planning (MRP) systems abound. Most platforms support several dozen competitive offerings. Narrow that list to client/server and most disappear. Narrow it even more to true client/server and the number drops to a couple. Developing true clients is proving costly and difficult.

Let me go back and define my terms. A true client to me handles presentation and logic. When I have a 486, Pentium, or PowerPC I want it to do more than play $4,000 dumb terminal.

Most OO expert system shells ship as true client/server products. Sure you can run the engine on a minicomputer or mainframe, but the important versions run on Macs, PCs, and UNIX workstations. Query the server, then process the results in local memory with the local CPU. That to me, is a client. Maybe a look at object-oriented expert systems shells could speed lagging cross-platform clients to market.

2.0 Prototyping for 3GLs

When discussing the value of incremental development, objects, and other benefits of expert system development environments, it seems a bit funny to look at them as prototyping tools for third general languages. The truth is most C-based expert systems on the market started out as LISP or Prolog. Once the concepts were down, they transformed into the more politically correct (and profitable) C. I have prototyped many an idea using an expert system shell, just to show a quick result. If LISP was the prototyping language for a C program, why not use the prototyping abilities inherited from LISP to prototype new applications and business processes. Buttons, windows, logic, debugging, and out of the box client/server. What more do you need for a prototype?

1.0 Graphical Development Environment

Expert system shells provide fully integrated development environments: rule editors, dictionaries, documentation fields, debuggers, and graphical trees of rules and objects. I for one never want to see a command line again or type in the word *compile* or *link*. Of course, that is fantasyland, but when I'm working in a shell, that's what it feels like. If C++ were only this cool.

Number 11.0! Number 11.0!

AI systems provide many advantages when developing client/server applications. Many of those benefits derive from the close linkage of rules and objects. Although the benefits are important, AI technology is nowhere near as standardized as C or Pascal. The concepts translate from product to product, but the implementation of concepts is wildly divergent. Feature divergence, alas, is the subject for another article.

If you choose a product like ART*Enterprise, Nexpert Object, ADS, or ProKappa, you will realize these ten benefits. Inference, Neuron Data, Trinzic, and IntelliCorp spent many hours delivering client/server computing before it stood alongside business process reengineering as a definitive term for the '90s. You can mix and match GUI tools, database access tools, and various languages, or you can take advantage of the integrated environments delivered by the AI community. These tools won't bring consciousness to your applications, but they may very well make your customers sit up and take notice.

And hey, if these aren't reason enough to use AI, I can always twist your sensibilities with Gillooly GUIs, Bobbit bindings, and Princess Di demons. Hell, maybe we could even discuss the concept of Letterman literals.

MIS INTELLIGENCE

AI people like to solve big problems. We like to look like heroes. We often perform great acts of heroism to solve business problems, often at the expense of our own organization. AI is an ad hoc profession with little agreement on formal ways of using tools and concepts. Researchers in machine intelligence find new ways of mimicking human thought each day.

Current commercial AI tools reflect old research technology that is focused more on delivering business savings than on intelligent computers. Yet the rudimentary intelligence of these systems is ideal for certain applications, not the least of which focuses us inward on our own expertise: navigating data and writing queries. With the move to client/server computing information technology customers want more and more control of their information destiny, often without the background or knowledge to take advantage of relationships between data. They may write poorly formed queries that thrash through databases like electronic thunderstorms, producing chaotic results, or they may write well formed queries that ask the wrong questions. The time has come to put our tools to work for ourselves. The requests for new cuts of corporate data will overwhelm us unless we leverage our own expertise.

Many organizations are moving to relational databases as their strategic platform and building data warehouses to simplify and combine scattered data. In the old days, this data belonged to customers, but it always came cloaked in the garb of MIS. We printed reports and dropped them into bins, ready for a user to pick them up and rekey them into spreadsheets. We created screen-based reports to make the information available on demand. Our customers are smarter now. They know there are better ways—and ways that don't depend on a call to MIS for the inevitable response: "Take a number; we'll get to you soon."

The hype about direct Structured Query Language (SQL) access to databases has given our customers the view that an afternoon class in SQL will prepare them to unleash their wildest information fantasies on our unsuspecting databases. SQL presents a deceptively simple demeanor. Graphic user interfaces to databases, tables, and tuples propagate the myth of simplicity. Displaying tables as pictures isn't going to reduce the underlying model to MacPaint lucidity. Data warehouses and other extract schemes can reduce complexity, but for large sets of data, nothing substitutes for a firm grasp of relational database issues. Relational databases come from a long line of logical reasoning and theory. Performance realities force data duplication and non-normalized implementations—strange fields and keys that mean little to people not caught in the challenge of database efficiency and durability. Capturing and distributing our intelligence is the best way to help our customers navigate the legacy of our internal Infobahns.

Tools like Trinzic's Forest & Trees and ClearAccess's ClearAccess provide end users with direct access to data. They embed knowledge into canned queries. Ad hoc queries require people to understand relational subtleties they may not be prepared for. Information miners need to know SQL to make these tools dig the holes they want dug. Anybody can get data out of a single table, but try teaching a purchasing clerk how to write an outer join with a half twist. No telling what gyrations your database engine will go through. And even if you can get data from a table, which table has the information?

Finally, the intelligence part. AionDS, Nexpert, Kappa, and ART*Enterprise connect to relational databases. The tools need not be limited to support a specific business application. Placing the collective wisdom of your database management team into an expert system will be a boon to information technology customers searching for better ways to search for data. Expert database systems can be used as direct links to databases or to optimize user queries. They translate data between production databases and a warehouse or decision support system.

Expert query systems aren't as visible as tools that stifle credit card fraud, but they increase productivity by allowing purchasing, sales, and accounting personnel and by delivering needed information concisely and accurately, leaving people time to concentrate on their real jobs. Getting data out of a database should not require a degree in logic and relational theory—at least on the part of the consumer. Think about that purchasing clerk squinting through thick bifocals, nose pressed against a thirteen-inch VGA monitor, and trying to figure out which table has late POs in it. Sure, the clerk may only go through that once, twice, twenty times, but it can be avoided altogether with expert assistance.

Why am I discussing data access at this point in the discussion? Because objects are they key. Model each database and each attribute as objects. Previously I have discussed how rules manipulate objects. By encoding the knowledge about data structures you can select which elements are relevant, order them correctly, and turn them into an SQL call string, throw the string toward the database engine, and wait for the result. Sounds simple, doesn't it? Well ...

Is It That Simple?

From the technology point of view, yes and no. Yes, it is a simple matter to map databases to objects. Various tools make the mapping more or less a chore. ART*Enterprise facilitates the process with its global schema capture tools, others require hand coding or interfacing with a CASE tool. Creating the rules, however, will take some time. There is nothing prohibitive about this, I've done it. It just takes time.

From the organization standpoint, it is not so easy. Many organizations pride themselves in rapid deployment of new databases or the staying power of their legacy systems. Most have realized the mess they have created and are taking interim steps, like creating data warehouses, to bridge the gap between dirty data days and the future facilitated by controlled, consistent, and clean data. This mass of inconsistent data disallows global intelligence—small, focused knowledgebases may prove financially feasible alternatives to global propositions. Even if your shop is CASE driven, rapid changes sometimes bypass the process. CASE-based physical schema description becomes meaningless when meddling hands disturb the physical schema.

Let's take a look at a company in transition. They are putting up data warehouses. Information from legacy applications and new applications is being massaged and placed into a congruent and consistent format. The data elements mean the same thing all the time, and the relationships between tables are clear and constructed. Clear and constructed to its designers, that is, but our purchasing clerk remains confused.

IF request_var = "Late P.O.s" THEN attach LPO_TABLE to SELECTED TABLE_CLASS.[1]

This is a simple rule, but it already demonstrates the value of the concept. The clerk searches for a full concept that is meaningful. The rule finds the correct table. Along with this rule will be rules for which databases don't have relationships, which keys are built from other elements, and how to correctly write outer joins with a half twist. Building rules, like all things in AI, can be incremental. You can take advantage of the tested knowledge about one set of data while forming the next set of knowledge fragments.

AI also lets us use different names for different audiences without redefining databases or creating views. It allows for synonyms and antonyms. If you're reading this book, you already know objects allow for richer definitions than tables. In fact, selecting a particular attribute, rather than firing another rule, might fire a method or demon that would select other attributes that are defined as always being associated with the initial selection. Selecting part and quantity, for instance, might automatically choose unit of measure. Ten thousand feet of wire is a great deal different than ten thousand wheels of wire.

Once the process of specifying the required information is complete, the objects can be evaluated and ordered. The SQL statement can be formed and checked. But there are catches—and they are us.

Naming Things

A key element in constructing intelligent search tools is maintaining a consistent naming convention, and a consistent meaning. MCC's CYC project starts off with the concept of Thing. I like Thing. I like Stuff. The Carnot project at MCC uses CYC's knowledge as its representation of the real world. It uses CYC to understand queries and to understand databases. I have seen CYC perform on-the-fly database analysis, mapping tables and columns into its known data, and asking for help only when it gets stuck. When CYC becomes commercially available, it may be an option for all of us. In the meantime, we need to create our own worldview.

Let's take Stuff as a high-order grouping. It doesn't mean much, and it means a lot. If one says stuff, people think of physical things. I have stuff. I have things. Oh, things. Well, maybe CYC is right. Things are a higher grouping. Anything can be a thing: a word, an idea, an action, a pencil or a database. There are lots of kinds of things that also fall into groupings.

That sounds like class hierarchies, and it is. I come to object-oriented ideas via Things and Stuff, but most OO applications don't start with them. We start with Widget or Inventory, Employee or Transaction. We start with something familiar—something tangible to the task at hand—and drive down from there. Most OO systems today have little relationship between each other. Creating a good class hierarchy requires a touch of philosophy and a smattering of linguistics. New classes should require context for their relationships between ideas and, yes, things.

When we start at those low levels of naming, we are prone to choose a new starting point for an abstraction. Even with naming conventions and naming standards, you don't necessarily maintain a common level of abstraction. Large environments like Smalltalk help because you can see what came before, if you like. With C++ or CLOS, you often start out fresh. With a global hierarchy, we know the meaning of things and their relationships before we start. Each element is carefully placed in context of previous ideas. We can drill down from a new point, which instantly codifies the new direction and reinforces the previous hierarchy. We expand, we don't reinvent. New hierarchies add detail to the global web of concepts.

To succeed in creating global structures for naming data elements, each enterprise needs to choose its own starting point. Something so high that everything else conceivable fits into it. I think Morticia and Gomez would be happy. I can see a lot of Things being born.

Name That Tune

It is important to remember that MIS is a business. We have our own processes to worry about, not just those of our customers. If we can get our names in order, we can share our knowledge of data with our customers, freeing them to explore their information. Bringing intelligent search to the network achieves several of AI's goals. It distributes intelligence and it preserves knowledge—it also makes the knowledge visible, maintainable, and explicit.

We can go on frustrating our customers by keeping the rules about data to ourselves, or we can use our tools to make our intelligence more available to them. Eventually large intelligences like CYC will make getting an information nugget as easy as asking our neighbor for the time. But until then we need to invest our time in codifying our own intelligence. It's the smart thing to do.

KNOWLEDGE, REUSE, AND CHANGE

Components interchange. That is their value. If component interfaces remain constant, then components can be interchanged with those of like functionality or with newer components that correct errors or improve performance. And of course, components can be reused. Components have brought us high performance carburetors and heavy-duty shock absorbers, ceramic teeth, and tofu cheese. Automobile manufacturers reuse designs regularly. My Pontiac Grand Am is a sporty version of the Chevy Cavalier. The Buick Skylark and Oldsmobile Achieva also share a basic frame, drive train, and other components with my car. We look for economies of scale, but we also build from what we know. Mental models dictate our view of things—that is why even if you don't own a Grand Am, you would have no problem identifying it as a car.

It is precisely our worldview that makes component reuse possible. Many things seem immutable. Those things make excellent candidates for reuse. In software we find everything from interface widgets to date conversion routines to methods for balancing inventory. Objects also represent things and ideas. The CAD representation of a shock absorber is as reusable as the shock absorber itself.

In the realm of knowledge, how we do things often seems as unchangeable as the products we make or the tools we use. But reengineering challenges our assumptions. Business process reengineering is really not much different than reinvention or revolution. All three change fundamental views of things and ideas. The French Revolution changed political ideologies as well as economic reality of both commoner and aristocrat. The reinvention of communications from hand delivery to electronic delivery changed fundamental assumptions: information dissemination times collapsed from relaxed gait to the speed of light. Software built on obsolete assumptions becomes obsolete.

The Volatility of Knowledge

Personal knowledge bases change daily. To develop a competition analysis agent about the automobile industry, I would gather sources, list competitors, and write rules about how they are analyzed and what conclusions experts draw from their experience. I can build objects that know how to tap the information sources and display results. Competitor objects drive queries; results cause another wave of inquiry.

Now let us suppose we are in the United States in 1950. Ford, Chrysler, GM, and a handful of European car companies exist. The major U.S. manufacturers own the market. An expert system written in 1950 represents data from magazines, newspapers, and industry reports. Data would be reinput from paper subscriptions, except for the transcribed notes on industry gossip. Cars are large, heavy, and powerful.

If we move to 1980, the U.S. manufacturers, though still strong, are seriously challenged by Japanese and Korean competitors on price and quality. Market share is eroding. Paper-based information is quickly giving way to microtargeted electronic queries. Marketing and finance strategies are evolving. Small is in, big is out. The key is economy of size and gasoline consumption.

Reading this in 1998, you know that the automobile market is much different than it was in 1980. American-labeled automobiles have surged again in both market share and quality. Huge partnerships between U.S. manufacturers and the Japanese and European competitors redefine the meaning of domestic and foreign. Moderation between size and features rules the credit-burdened consumer.

From 1950 to 1998 knowledge about the automobile market and the knowledge about how to analyze it changed dramatically. An expert system written in 1950 would be useless in 1998. Manual entries would be replaced by electronic interfaces. Competitors and sources would be very different. Heuristics about consumer wants and needs, government regulations, geopolitical relationships, and other knowledge elements negate underlying structures and representations. Very little, if anything, from a 1950's expert system could be reused in 1998.

Knowledge is very volatile. I don't want to imply that knowledge cannot be reused. For a given period of time knowledge elements might very well be reusable across systems. But just as we reach stability, we challenge reuse through reengineering efforts that actively rewrite assumptions and rework business processes. Change in the automobile industry was anything but voluntary. Even if people and organizations resist change instead of encouraging it, things will change.

Managing Change with Reuse

Later in this chapter I will discuss the persistence of data. Here the relevancy of methods comes into question. The question is not necessarily one of reuse, but one of change management. Many of our basic assumptions about things reflect transitory lock-ins of technology or economies. Professor Brian Arthur of the Sante Fe Institute sees economics as nearly living systems that evolve much like life. Periods of stability follow periods of great change. Stephen Jay Gould calls a similar biological phenomenon punctuated equilibrium. For periods of equilibrium, reuse is viable, cost effective, and time saving. When things change, though, assumptions shatter.

Reuse has proffered from the graphic user interface (GUI). Widgets and the processes that support them are perfect models for reuse. The introduction of the Apple Macintosh and its GUI set expectations. Motif, Windows, OS/2, and many other systems have provided alternative arrangements of GUI elements, but most share common metaphors: buttons, windows, dialog boxes, scroll bars, and pull-down menus. The behavior of these items varies in minor ways from implementation to implementation, but for the most part, anybody familiar with one GUI can operate in another.

The GUI standard drove other standards. OO languages were naturals. GUI building tools for cross-platform compilation brought standard APIs. Develop an application in Windows, deliver it on a Mac. With the exception of minor interface changes and elements related to runtime memory management, little needs changing. Knowledge encapsulated in a system remains the same from platform to platform. The GUI is "locked-in" for the moment.

Applications, however, are but a reflection of underlying knowledge. Change the way you manage inventory and the inventory application must change. Think of the implications of a move from cash accounting to accrual. Most accounting systems accommodate both, but the underlying knowledge and the external interfaces change dramatically depending on the choice. The conversion from one to another is punctuated by a month or so of chaos, not to mention frets about lost income and the IRS. Imagine an easier way to use computers, and GUIs become historical artifacts.

It is at the moment when our businesses, our lives, or our world meets the edge of chaos that knowledge management becomes most important. A struggle ensues between maintaining the old equilibrium and embracing the opportunity found in change. The victory of change results in painful chaos coexisting with an increasingly anachronistic set of procedures, policies, and assumptions. Knowledge once considered immutable becomes history. Change always wins.

Historical evidence in both biology and economics indicates a high degree of correlation between adaptability and survival. When things change individuals and businesses need to change with them. Software systems must adapt as well. Anticipating and embracing change readies individuals and organizations for its inevitability.

In knowledge-based systems, knowledge management modules elevate rules from process to data. Experts enter knowledge through a case-based reasoning interface or rule-generating interface. Browsers help search for rules that experts can change. Many of these interfaces incorporate testing mechanisms to evaluate the impact of changing rules of the validity or performance of the system. Although these interfaces may prove unable to adapt to major changes in environment, they help cushion minor shifts and can sustain applications through periods of chaos while new applications develop.

The maxim that maintenance is the phase of software engineering most often forgotten is as true for knowledge-based systems as it is for conventional applications. Knowledge management modules are rare. Most expert system developers choose to ignore maintenance, rushing headlong into delivery. Extremely fragile knowledge-based systems that are sensitive to change result. Some projects hire knowledge engineers to maintain delicate rules relationships. Either choice is expensive; both have their utility depending on the volatility and complexity of the knowledge. Failure to fund any maintenance results in the even more costly fate of disuse. After an initial influx of knowledge ages, unmaintained expert systems become invalid.

The volatility of knowledge makes knowledge reuse a myth over extended periods of time. For short periods knowledge may well find its way into multiple systems. Most expert systems, however, exist in isolation eschewing any chance of reuse. Where expert systems do have companions, they probably share few standard elements beyond those also found in algorithmic applications (like GUI widgets).

Unlike other expert systems, diagnostic systems offer more chances for reuse. Diagnostic systems will always diagnose known problem sets on a finite population. A phone switch diagnostic application, for instance, will always diagnose problems with a given set of like configured switches. Diagnostic systems find reuse in evolutionary, modular technologies where some components remain the same, although the overall configuration changes. Revolutionary changes in phone switch technology, however, would invalidate the entire knowledge base. For the end user, adopting a new phone switch supplier would also invalidate any lessons learned about a previous brand.

Even if knowledge were pristine and invariable, the technology around it is likely to change. Copy libraries written in COBOL 68 don't incorporate well into Smalltalk or C++ environments. Although Smalltalk and C++ seem the preeminent champions of reuse, nothing guarantees their length of service. New languages develop regularly, and one or more may displace them. Changes in underlying knowledge forces rearrangement of interfaces, if not wholesale replacement of applications.

Codified knowledge reflects an instant in time. Knowledge is not immutable. Personal and world frameworks evolve even if we defy change. Punctuated equilibrium gives us moments of stability in which we can settle into a set of assumptions, create components, and reuse our components. Each of our assumptions runs, however, on a different clock. Any system element, from application languages to user interface metaphors, from underlying knowledge to computer hardware, could change without relation to other system elements. Rapid information technology means all applications constantly teeter on the edge of chaos.

Experts in all facets of the business need to remain cognizant of subtle changes in environment and communicate those changes to each other. They need to explore various scenarios and prepare for many of them. The best buffer to change remains communication. A good software budget doesn't hurt either. Any organization that believes application systems can go smoothly from development to maintenance, from operation to graceful retirement, ignores the inevitability of change.

Nature teaches a final reuse lesson by capitalizing on existing characteristics in unintended ways. Overgrown insulating scales on dinosaurs become feathers. The human voice, evolved for grunts and chortles, becomes an instrument of song. The wrist bone of a panda serves as an alternative to an already employed fifth digit.

Perhaps the best reuse we can imagine comes from seeing the potential in libraries and toolboxes. A graphics routine designed for mechanical analysis may be a great component for an executive information system. With an Intel Pentium computer the executive views data as an interactive contour chart. The routine, intended for a CAD workstation, finds new life because PCs evolved from slow 286 machines to CAD workstation-quality Pentium processors over the life of the component. Intent should not constrain use. In knowledge and in software, reuse proves most effective when we subdue our assumptions and find new uses for known things.

RETHINKING AI

A few years ago I wrote a pounding indictment of Roger Penrose's book, *The Emperor's New Mind*. I have mellowed a bit since then, but it is from redirecting my pen from frivolous misconceptions toward important issues. Penrose's attack on AI was directed at the misdirected. When Penrose called the strong AI community before him, much of what he said was true about their work. At the time of my review, I was defending colleagues and standing up for the cause. Now, however, I think we were all wrong in our approach and in our model of machine intelligence. I do not believe current AI research will lead to thinking machines.

So what now, the Object Magazine AI columnist is abandoning AI? Not at all. I believe machines will indeed gain a type of intelligence, but I am far from omniscient and cannot predict what form that intelligence will take. I do know, however, that machine evolution is highly diverged from our own and has seen as many fits and starts as our ancestors did on the plains of Africa. This unique path combined with unique inputs ultimately created a worldview so different from ours that a machine is incapable of sharing much of anything cognitive with us. The shear complexity of components will someday manifest itself in a new intelligence, not a mimicry of our egocentric view of intelligence, but something entirely different. In some ways, as we already know, computers will beat us hands down at mathematics and we will continue to prevail in human-oriented arts. Machines will not be better overall than their creators, they will be different. In fact, our frame of reference may well make it impossible to recognize the intelligence of the machine. Computers will fail the Turing test not because they are not worthy, but because the test is examining the wrong factors. That we are the only "intelligent" life we know, does not mean we or the universe is incapable of creating a different type of intelligence.

We make the assumption that our success as a species is unique to our intelligence. Close examination of history and archeology shows our intelligence is an adaptive compensation for physical weaknesses. Our measly million-year existence as a species pales before "less evolved" creatures that adapt with fangs or teeth or swiftness. So far they have been more successful than humanity when it comes to natural selection.

Carnegie Mellon's Hans Morevec believes our evolution is tied to that of the machine. It is possible that the machine will replace us wholesale in the future as we merge our intelligence with a machine's superior physical and environmental adaptation. I think it is more likely that we will coexist with machines and form a symbiotic relationship. Human evolution will continue along its mental path with new deviations that will help us communicate better with our swift inventions.

Given this framework, the idea that we will imbue human intelligence to machines is somewhat an insult to the machine. Computers are finely tuned for things that we do not do and ill equipped for understanding our conceptual framework. Think about how hard it is to emulate a 68040 on a PowerPC chip. Motorola developed both and Apple wrote software for both, yet the differences in instruction sets, I/O, and other factors result in emulated performance that is always less than native performance. The same holds true of emulating humans in computers. No matter what we do, the performance will always be inferior to whatever native intelligence emerges.

As you read this section, you will see little that expands your understanding of how computers are learning to reason as we do. Instead you will find many techniques manifested in different architectures, on different platforms, and in different languages. These are valuable techniques that allow some kinds of human knowledge to augment software applications. They do not, however, make these applications artificially intelligent. Even the most sophisticated of tools have no sense of their knowledge, no understanding of their learning, and no capability of clarification through a meaningful dialog with their instructors.

In some ways, however, computers in a broad sense are becoming more intelligent through their interactions and native complexity. Phone switches and large computer networks that route traffic and manage data flow show more intelligence than a diagnostic or scheduling expert system. It is not the kind of intelligence that will win the Turing test; it is an intelligence that is very different than what humans desire to do or are capable of doing.

Ours is not the only intelligence. Ours is not the only means of survival. If our electro-mechanical offspring are to evolve, isn't it likely that as they become more capable their evolution will take place in ways we do not direct? Since computers have not yet evolved a philosophy, then I leave these thoughts to my human readers to ponder for now.

From Philosophy to Commercial Practicalities

The latest in commercial AI is that AI companies have transformed themselves into client/server front-end suppliers. Very little has changed in the reasoning engines of these tools over the past several years. In fact, a majority of tools in the "Intelligent Objects Buyer's Guide" in this book all use the decades old RETE algorithm for pattern matching in the inference engine. Some are faster, some are more flexible, and many include elaborate development environments. Under the hood, though, not much is new.

There is nothing wrong with these tools. As corporations move toward knowledge management to support their non-algorithmic processes, knowledge management is coming into vogue again. We don't call it AI and we combine it with groupware, but somewhere an inference engine is likely involved.

All of the tools listed in the "Intelligent Objects Buyer's Guide" are good at capturing the logic of the human mind and running it consistently, without error, over and over again. The problem is that human thought is much more complex than can be represented in RETE or any other inference engine. Although some other reasoning models exist, none of the recent research, from Cog, to CYC to Soar has made it to the commercial market. case-based reasoning has been implemented, along with neural nets and dedicated pattern matches. No integrated framework has yet found its way to the commercial market, so these techniques are often used independently.

I hear rumors that some of these new reasoning tools and their associated knowledge bases may be making it to market. Cycorp is testing industry for commercial applications of Doug Lenat's decade-old CYC and its thousands of axioms and dozens of inference methods. Soar and its flexible reasoning engine are rumored to be finding a commercial implementation.

Even if new techniques emerge, they will have a difficult time finding their way into corporate tool kits. This is not a field of instant wins and quick adoption. Those days have already come and gone. Even the most sophisticated of AI applications finds it difficult to muster but a handful of adherents. Keep watching though. The first wave of techniques was powerful and continues to perform. The next wave may not generate the same enthusiasm, but its techniques will be several times more expressive at their representation of knowledge and much more flexible in how they reason about that knowledge.

The next generation of tools will be no more artificially intelligent that the current stable of products, but they will be useful and should not be ignored.

The Death of Frames

If shipping tools have not challenged our minds, they have challenged their own roots. As I examined the products and literature from the broad survey of tools that combine rules and objects, I found the movement away from traditional frames a telling one. Frames originated from the AI community as ways of representing classified facts in a hierarchy and capturing values in slots and behaviors in demons or methods. Several of the tools in the survey continue to use frames implemented in a variety of proprietary ways. None of the proprietary systems can share values directly with one another without the intervention of an API.

Some tools, however, now use CLOS or C++ for knowledge representation. This technique provides a common memory space that can be shared by heuristic and algorithmic processes. Over the years I have distinguished the history of frames from that of objects and discussed their semantic differences, but for practical reasons my conclusions always lead to the analysis that it does not matter which you choose.

Now I think it matters in commercial tools as they exist today, and it matters that those tools use open and standard representations. The tools that use C++ and come delivered as class libraries afford a great deal more openness than their more proprietary peers. Rather than master another syntax and another semantics, C++ programmers can concentrate on developing meaningful and reusable C++ representations and then reasoning over them from inference engines stored in classes rather than outside code.

The C++ inference engines, however, often lack the niceties of the more mature tools with their elaborate development environments and debugging facilities. But since C++ is evolving its own tool support, these classes may find their graphic development environments coming from third parties as a C++ environment component. Programmers can concentrate on efficient reasoning over a universe of C++ and leave the GUI to companies like Microsoft and Centerline.

A Few Thoughts on AI in the Early '90s

AI remains in the doldrums when compared to the new technology upstarts like the Internet, Web browsers, and groupware. The AI techniques found in the '60s, '70s, and '80s, though, remain valid and valuable. As companies realize they need staff trained in the liberal arts to bring adaptability to their corporate culture, they may also need software that can produce the best answer, if not the only answer, from a sea of conflicting inputs. Knowledge-based software generates approximate answers, but the technology remains inherently difficult to implement given knowledge ownership issues with experts and the non-traditional time frames involved in interviews, prototyping and constant, and endless maintenance.

It is the goal of true AI believers to reduce the non-software elements by creating systems of sufficient complexity that they will carry on a conversation with an expert, and through trial and error learn the ropes of a process or task. No such luck yet. Even the largest and most comprehensive of research projects has yet to realize what it is or what it is for, let alone how to improve upon itself without the fine hand of programmers and knowledge engineers hand-tweaking both its knowledge and its inference engine. And as I pointed out in the beginning of this section, the goals of human mimics may be a disservice to both use and computers.

To be fair, the companies listed here and the articles about intelligent software are not in the business of creating thinking software.

They are in the business of selling tools to software developers that provide certain capabilities, in most cases knowledge representation and inference. In this regard all of them are established companies with products that will produce exciting possibilities once they find homes in corporate software arsenals.

THE PERSISTENCE OF INTELLIGENCE

Now let's explore object-oriented databases. If persistent objects are to do more than their SQL brethren do, then they will require behaviors, and some of those behaviors will represent organizational knowledge. Coding an intelligent system without acknowledging both data and knowledge is a mistake. Sophisticated procedures in objects—especially those deployed in work management and in agent technology—capture, retain, and distribute organizational knowledge. They embody facts and processes about the way things are done.

And the way things are done in most corporations is not only varied, but also volatile. In the world of straight algorithm, such as payroll, we often think of simple formulas that deduct our taxes, leaving us with net income. As the year draws to a close I feel for all those systems analysts assigned to payroll system modifications. Not only do state and federal agencies turn out reams of tax law modifications, but the myriad choices in cafeteria-style supplemental benefits, like medical and dental coverage, add new twists to the decades end-of-year rewrite of payroll. There will be no rest until January.

Payroll is a good example of annual volatile knowledge. The shifts of knowledge within corporations, however, is not so scheduled nor so well documented. And because it is not governed by regulation or watched by each employee at the end of the week, it is much more abstract and hidden. Discoveries happen; procedures change. The rapidity of change in modern corporations makes knowledge so dynamic and transient that intelligent systems are nearly obsolete the day they are installed. Tools like case-based reasoning minimize recoding of formal rules, but they do not negate the investment in knowledge identification and refinement.

So like all software, the intelligence we express as rules and procedures requires maintenance. Some maintenance can be planned out by carefully following good software practice, like writing clear specifications, making good design choices, or documenting the system. The change-generating phenomenon arises from the nature of knowledge itself: it never stops increasing, finding synergy, or becoming obsolete.

AI Ain't Different

Knowledge engineers rapidly prototyping systems often find themselves engaged in culture battles with their more formal, structured colleagues. They find it annoying to follow standard software practices. The truth is, that for the most part, AI ain't different. An expert system involves coding some fragment of human knowledge into digital form that is executable, over and over again, in some kind of CPU. The mystery of higher-order thought and its complexity should not negate standard practices, but make them all the more important. The more complex a system, the more difficult it is to understand it without documentation.

Intelligent systems should require a design that defines enough of the product to make knowledge-base design issues and inference mechanism choices. It requires considerable effort, for instance, to move from a rule-based environment to a more object-oriented model. The choice of inference engine features being used also constrains or expands a project's scope. By making backward, forward, or mixed-mode choices early, the design of knowledge can be more consistent and scalable. You know how to structure the knowledge because you know how it will be processed.

Another realm of explicit documentation and design comes from the interaction of the intelligent system with other applications. As corporations move from mainframes to client/server architectures, standard systems like finance and manufacturing are often in a state of flux. Understanding how an intelligent system reads and writes data, and how it interacts with other application processes, can mean the difference between flexible interfaces and a system that becomes unmaintainable when its original source of data ceases to exist.

Along with understanding interfaces to other applications, an intelligent system's place within a business process needs to be understood. With rampant business process reengineering efforts underway, a process once supported by an intelligent system may be eliminated completely or reengineered to the point that a knowledge base interacting with the system is no longer applicable. Business process re-engineering deals with restructuring the fundamental knowledge of a corporation. Each change can mean hours of new knowledge acquisition and recoding.

To make maintenance less stressful, if not more enjoyable, people leading intelligent system projects need to document all aspects of a system with detail and clarity. Class hierarchies, rule interactions, application interfaces, variable definitions, and other attributes require concise and vigorous documentation.

Focusing Inward

And then there is the intelligent application itself. Rapid prototyping often means that the final prototype becomes the production system. It is common to find expert systems that grow from a few rules to a few hundred with little documentation of the knowledge acquired or the representation choices. One of the biggest challenges in knowledge engineering is passing on knowledge from original knowledge engineer to the person or team maintaining the application.

Knowledge systems maintenance is as much about maintaining team lore as it is about maintaining the application itself. It is about context and knowing why choices were made. All knowledge-based systems are fragile entities with edges so definite that pushing beyond their constraints can result in answers that may not only be meaningless, but also dangerous. Expert systems for nuclear plants or process facilities make real-time determinations about action within potentially explosive situations. Knowing what causes a system to make a decision is of the utmost importance. Not knowing, at the time a change occurs, or even worse, an error, will be a costly learning experience.

All systems evolve over time. Algorithms change and data elements get renamed. Cosmetic and structural changes abound. Knowledge systems change not only as a result of known policy changes written down and handed out by corporate bureaucrats or government lawmakers. Knowledge systems are susceptible to external changes that invalidate the knowledge to knowledge known but unarticulated and to subtle personal changes that cause an expert to rethink his or her own knowledge about something.

As of yet, no expert system can rethink its basic assumptions. With case-based reasoning expert systems acquire new facts and make new inferences about a well-defined domain, but they can neither discover new attributes nor discard current ones. What the programmer says is important is always important.

The arrival of Microsoft's Windows 95 shook corporate knowledge-bases. Although Windows 95 is still Windows, its new interface and architecture almost completely negated any knowledge captured about Windows 3.1, by humans or computers. Experts were no longer experts, cases in help desk systems no longer applied. Corporations had to spend months returning to the same level of competence they achieved with Windows 3.1. And the transition knowledge that links Windows 95 to Windows 3.1 became unnecessary almost as soon as it was mastered.

The dilemma of relearning Windows does provide a concrete example of how quickly knowledge can become obsolete. What looked valuable yesterday—what seemed persistent and reliable—turns to rubble in corporate and personal memory. Not only do we need to continue to learn, we need to continue to teach our colleagues and the systems we rely on.

When we focus inward we must look at the expert system in its context, as a piece of the enterprise's knowledge infrastructure. And we must document the *whys* and *whats* assumed and the *whys* and *whats* implemented in a system. We must maintain the knowledge by maintaining the link to its source. By asking the expert or experts what they think they have learned, that will augment knowledge or evolve it.

In essence, the expert system becomes a team member ready to absorb new knowledge, ready to learn. In the persistence of knowledge, you cannot find a more receptive student than an expert system. But as a hand-coded application, the new knowledge must integrate well with what has come before. Without adequate documentation and a firm grasp of the system's structure, the new knowledge may not find a home, or it could turn a production system into dysfunctional code. All team members, from knowledge engineer to expert, must make every effort to plan for the inevitability of new knowledge.

Reawakenings

Salvador Dali's *Persistence of Memory* shows a world melted by the realization that time is not a constant. And like time, its close relative, change, eludes our most scientific efforts to predict its rate or direction. We cannot jump forward to see what will come or know how current actions will influence the future. Perhaps our best architecture is fluid and learns not so much the rote facts and processes of the mind, but its infinite ability to mold to the moment.

It is a myth that expert systems replace people. Intelligent systems only know as much as we are willing to tell them. They then represent that knowledge. They take what was, at a moment in time, the epitome of a domain, and deliver it consistently and reliably. For the expert, the phone rings a few less times a day, allowing him or her to retain a knowledge edge. The intelligent system, in the mean time, is transferring the expert's knowledge to the less skilled, in fits and flashes connected to real events. The knowledge not only perpetuates, it spreads.

Today we are moving toward a model that combines knowledge and data. We are turning once transitory objects into permanent and persistent members of the business community, coexisting with their Oracle, Sybase, and IMS counterparts. And with that permanence, we must deal with the transitory nature of both the data and the behaviors. Our monolithic object hierarchies build on assumptions constantly challenged by economics, management direction, and experience.

If we want objects of intelligence to be successful, we must acknowledge that persistence does not mean permanence. In both data and process, it is more important to capture the context of knowledge that discerns the relevant from the irrelevant. Not only does the world change around us, but more and more we partake in proactive efforts to accelerate and transform the change. As organizations supplement transactions and operational systems with intelligent applications, we will need to spend an increasing amount of time pondering our own ponderings. Only in an open environment ready to accept change can we accept people, and systems, talking to themselves about their own meaning, their own place in the scheme of things.

THE PROBLEM WITH PERSISTENCE

As we learn to store more information in persistent repositories, we will experience a problem with digital information that we do find in our own chaotic consciousness. We have yet to develop tools that differentiate much beyond patterns and simple strings. Even when crude rules add to the search, they do not have sufficient knowledge to validate the relevance of returned data. As the available data increases, we will retrieve larger data sets with each query. The data of the world will be at our fingertips, but it will remain our task to interpret that data with our knowledge of the present. Computers do not forget. The amount of data increases daily. Persistence is a problem.

Everything Changes

In science classes around the world, Bohr's model of the atom continues to reign as a popular representation of atomic construction decades after physicists abandoned it as a viable model of depicting electrons and their orbits. Current models display electron particles and waves swirling in twisted orbits about the nucleus of the atom. For school children, Bohr's model remains a basic abstraction that teaches basic concepts. If the child chooses physics as a profession, they will retain Bohr as a historic representation and replace the ancient model with the one currently in vogue. And based on the pace of learning about atoms, they may very well repeat this time and again during their career.

Things do indeed change over time. Even the truths of science, documented by a preponderance of evidence at any single point in time, become the falsehoods of superstitious old folk as new explanations emerge.

Think about the transition from traditional ideas of our world's founding to scientific explanations based on geologic time and Darwinian evolution. Religious argument, Lamarckian evolution, and pre-Mendelian concepts of heredity no longer inform the enlightened. We reason about religious literature and early scientific explanations in the context of current understanding. We see them as history, but no longer relevant to discussions of current theory.

In everyday life the models we use may matter little if our life does not depend on them. In expert systems, however, lives and fortunes sometimes do depend on subtle changes in perspective. Stock market trading systems now find themselves off-line when the market behaves in a way their programmed perceptions cannot fathom. They start buying and selling based on their rules, but for the moment the rules prove irrelevant. The context has changed. And what of intelligent systems running a nuclear reactor?

The current state of commercial AI applies a small subset of knowledge to a small instance of data. If the context changes, the system has no ability to adapt its rules to the new reality. The limitations of data and knowledge are best understood when joined by information and wisdom.

Data, Information, Knowledge, and Wisdom

The information age. Information is everywhere. But that assumption is false. The essential element of this age is not information, but data. Data is raw material. Most of what we have stored in our brains and on our computers is data—in and of itself, inert and meaningless. Information arises from the application of knowledge to data. For a single instance, indeed for thousands of seemingly concurrent instances, data informs knowledge. Information then exists only at the point it informs. Once that act occurs, information either returns as new data for later retrieval or increases knowledge by providing the mind or program with new rules or other knowledge constructs.

In our mind knowledge is applied by wisdom, a kind of meta-knowledge that knows when to apply what reasoning to what data to make a proper interpretation. It is wisdom that learning systems strive for. AI makes it easy to amass rules. It is nearly impossible to coordinate a large knowledge space when confronted with a massive influx of data. Current reasoning engines must be explicitly programmed to change from one point of view to another. All points of view must be known and entered. There is no room for the reality of chaos.

Wisdom and knowledge act not only on data, but also act in a certain time and at a certain place. They contain spatial and temporal elements that arise from the senses. Intelligent applications to date have little sense of time or space. They act something like little brain damaged patients, unable to distinguish the present from the past. All available data appear to be of equal value.

True intelligence requires rapid context switching that places the current moment in perspective of past experience. Wisdom and knowledge define what we do with the incoming data. Our current experience is "informed" by our instantaneous interpretation of incoming data. We recognize it, we categorize it and we act on it—it adds to our short-term memories and triggers long-term memories. Over time, depending on the rules and patterns invoked, the data becomes bits, episodes, or reconfigures into new reasoning constructs.

The temporal dimension is almost never addressed in application systems, outside of those concerned with scheduling or simulation. Transaction systems rely on data to change over time. Inventory numbers change as issues and receipts from warehouses are processed; accounts payable wax and wane with the receipt of invoices and the mailing of checks. But in data that represents more than a simple state, time is very important.

The theories of science all still exist in their original tomes, some digitized for easy retrieval. Although Darwin still speaks in relevance based on observations made since the *Origin of Species*, Lamarck's writings provide perspective rather than fact. Reasoning systems must be able to recognize what is important to the question at hand, not simply regurgitate all available facts.

In transaction-oriented systems the data is simple. In knowledge-based systems the data may be complex and multifaceted. In fact complex data types is a primary selling point for object-oriented databases. When several complex options present themselves with equal resolution, it is only the application of knowledge, in the context of the present of wisdom, that can make the best interpretation of the data.

Persistence is a problem as the rate of data continues to grow without parallel growth in reasoning ability in systems. Text retrieval and database engines will divulge their contents in large chunks based on basic filters. The problem with persistence is that we must take on the chore of figuring out which data is relevant to our query based on age, time, quality, and other perspectives.

Reasoning About Persistent Objects

Let me stop here and actually discuss persistent objects. Object-oriented databases are sold because they represent the very complex data that I identified as growing to overwhelming proportions. Using some basic OO features before instantiating a database can help add the perception of context and make persistent databases more useful and manageable.

In AI the class can act as a consolidator of concepts by providing focus for a search. Using dynamic attachment, class can be moved from one temporal class to another, from one contextual class to another. With multiple inheritance the subclasses can be members of many metaclasses, adding to the complexity of the representation, but also adding to its richness.

Metaclasses may represent any abstract idea such as a year, a theory, or a location. Time and location combine to create time segments that can be searched for knowledge limited in scope to what is known at some time in some place. There is almost a time travel feel to these representations. If I code contemporary computing data, I can freely use the acronym PDA, with little confusion. My Sharp Zaurus near my right hand leaves little mystery about personal digital assistants. Turn back the clock to November 12, 1985 and computers are slow VisiCalc-wielding future door stops. Perhaps Alan Kay might recognize the concept of a PDA if you told him it was like a miniature version of his Dynabook.

Even shorter periods of time matter with persistence. Patient monitoring systems, stock selling and buying systems, manufacturing systems, and other time-oriented systems need context. In systems driven by complex, free-form data, like competitor analysis systems, the objects of the moment matter—but the object of the moment itself is a complex question. Is the current state of a competitor the most important place to focus? Perhaps it is the potential of a competitor as derived from the analysis of past performance that would yield better insight. Each instance of temporal context requires deep discussions about relevance and representation.

The implementation of multilevel, temporal memory models proves difficult without multiple inheritance. The shift from class to class forces inheritance of attributes that make an object more or less important in a given context. The ability to make these shifts, and indeed the engineering of the shifts in focus, present issues of knowledge representation. Shifts of attention also bring in ideas of chaotic configurations, where the complexity of the system gains a status of near self-organization. The implementers of the system can no longer test outcomes because the interaction of the processes and data achieve their own internal momentum and order.

Single inheritance systems have difficulty directing search via class attachment; multiple inheritance systems have the upper hand here. By attaching or detaching trees of objects from a class or set of classes, variables inherit values at runtime that provide better answers in a given context, and searches can be narrowed by say, searching the class of "darkness" vs. the class "day_light" in a security system. Many representations of the day lose their meaning in the evening's shadows. Rather than code a whole set of rules with a conditional statement searching for daylight or darkness, the attachment of objects to one class or the other drives the search from the data. As the objects change their behavior, the search engine "sees differently."

I am only sketching issues here. The persistence of complex objects, be they stored in OO databases or as files on a Web server, require analysis about their use over time and in complex queries that don't come up during more traditional systems analysis. Ignoring time and context abstracts problems to very manageable levels. The challenge to take advantage of the data and the best way to accomplish that is through thoughtful discourse on all of the issues surrounding it.

Additional Meditations

We, of course, are not always so fortunate as to eradicate our own parochialism from examining facts. Prejudice, preconception, wishfulness, ignorance, and narrow-mindedness exert themselves on our own interpretations. If we fail to imbue our software mimics with the power of context and focus, we will also be unable to give them those other less lofty attributes, thus relegating them forever to the retrieval of data in nearly raw, uninterpreted form. Even after applying a search for patterns a distracted human mind might fail to recognize, artificial intelligence would miss other subtle relationships that might lead to recombination and innovation.

In this age of persistent data we need not only filters to narrow the incoming data, but also knowledge to interpret the data and wisdom to drive the knowledge. Today we are the only source of wisdom.

Persistence is a problem. Information never ages because of its brief existence. Wisdom does not age because it is the representation of our personal evolution, learning constantly. Wisdom forgets the unimportant and dredges up memories as required. Our great concern with the digitalization of all data raises the questions of who will have enough time and enough wisdom to know, or care, what it all means.

IMMUTABLE KNOWLEDGE

In "Choruses from *The Rock*" T. S. Eliot asks:

> *Where is the wisdom we have lost in knowledge?*
> *Where is the knowledge we have lost in information?*

The constant onslaught of information forces me to ask these questions daily. Megabytes of e-mail assault multiple mailboxes. I wish for a clone ready to cull the important from the mundane. But when I reflect as poet and not as technologist, I wonder, as Eliot anticipated, how much we have given away in our thirst for information.

The other day I heard that a daily edition of the *New York Times* contains more information than an average person living in the Renaissance would encounter during their lifetime. I struggle to remain a computing generalist, but I now realize why doctors specialize. In the last ten years I forgot more than I learned the previous ten. I know more and more about less and less. Of course, that nearly makes me an expert since I will soon know so much that I will know absolutely everything about nothing.

Objects of Speculation

This issue's focus on object-oriented databases triggered my reflections on the wisdom of immutable knowledge. The brain, after all, is the best architected database ever created. Millions upon millions of connections between millions and millions of memories literally define our private universes—a universe of relationships. Many theorists believe objects and their semantics best mimic our organic representations. In his *Introduction to Object-Oriented Databases* (1990, The MIT Press), Won Kim stated that "The ability to represent and manipulate complex nested objects to allow the successive refinement of complex entities" was a primary feature of OO databases, however, often run at cross purposes with knowledge representation. Although I am a proponent of objects as the best representation method for the core of knowledge-based systems, it is important to recognize the basic fallacy of most object models in representing knowledge.

Let's see what Won Kim's next sentence shares: "It should be possible to fetch an entire complex object or a subset of it as a single unit, or incrementally one component object at a time."

Our consciousness is much more concerned with the relationship between objects than with the objects themselves. When we talk to knowledge, we talk about what something *means*. Meaning comes from placing some object, be it thing or idea, into a context. Contexts evolve from earlier contexts. We teach our children to refrain from touching the stove because it is HOT! Of course, that warning saves many a child from first-degree burns, but it is also a good example of forced context shifting as we try to teach them how to cook. The heat of the stove is only off limits until we develop the ability to understand a more complex relationship to the stove than NO! We unlearn the fear, retain the respect, and reorient the heat from the concept of pain to the concept of tool. That is a pretty complex transaction for even the most sophisticated OODBMS.

Fetching an object full blown or in pieces is certainly helpful in a manufacturing environment. Bills of material strain relational databases—it is as though object-oriented databases were designed with them in mind. IS-A and HAS-A relationships define most physical things well, but they are poor definitions for knowledge. And although object-oriented databases often support user defined relationships, their performance constraints make them meager support tools for representing complex knowledge.

Dr. Kim's sixth feature for next-generation database systems (the quotes above represent his first feature) states that although these systems should include inferencing mechanisms and efficient unification, most do not. It is difficult to keep up with the perceived complexity of a modern application without interjecting the complexity of thought processes and knowledge representation. There is little call among the keepers of highly complex physical information, multimedia objects, or software widgets for inferencing.

Paradise Lost?

Knowledge lost in information and wisdom lost in knowledge. We deceive ourselves that computer systems adequately represent the complexity of business processes, let alone the complexity of the human mind. Both the mind and our work environment constantly evolve object intersections that constantly change contexts.

A meeting of ten people changes ten views of the world, and because no one started at the same place, or stayed through the entire meeting or paid attention to the same points, or brought with them the same knowledge for interpreting the new data, no one in that meeting was affected in the same way. The personal representations of the world make the interpersonal representations even more complex because no third party can adequately understand or predict the interactions or conclusions of two colleagues, no matter how well they know each other.

Our pursuit of data and our concentration on transforming that data into information often forces us to ignore the implication of the information. The shear amount of information also stops us from incorporating that information into our personal knowledge base. And if we do not internalize knowledge, then we cannot share it. If we do share unincorporated knowledge, it is like spitting out facts for no reason. We do not retain a context.

In the human mind, and in organizations, wisdom is the ultimate context. Wisdom defines what knowledge we apply and, thus, how we choose the path toward the incorporation of information and data.

The more we save stuff in computer databases, no matter how sophisticated those databases are, the more we believe our computer systems are capable of informing us. We apply complex tools to large data sets and "mine" knowledge from the relationships between the information.

Data mining is actually a good recognition of our relationship between data and ourselves. Data mining acknowledges that we do not understand the rules related to the data we enter. Knowledge hides from the creator of data. And the computer system that stores the data is equally unaware of the patterns concealed in its physical structure. The results of the data mining, of course, mean nothing without human recognition and confirmation of the conclusions.

Object-oriented databases understand their contents no better than their relational cousins. OODBMS products represent data more organically and allow for more fluid navigation, but they represent only an incremental improvement in knowledge representation because the storage and retrieval mechanisms still require arduous coding, especially with the introduction of user defined relationships.

In fact knowledge and wisdom are not lost so much as neglected. Our information age is more an age of data. Information to me exists only at the brief moment knowledge recognizes data. At that moment we have the choice of interacting with the data, changing it to create new data, or to incorporate the information in a way that it becomes knowledge. Our culture drives us toward the former. Our focus so often turns to the creation of data during the recognition with information that we fail to incorporate the data's knowledge potential.

Searching for Knowledge and Wisdom

After I watch an imaged brain recall a memory, I cannot define knowledge, memory, or information in a way that would allow me to write a system specification that could be coded into a digital computer.

If you have read my articles in *Object Magazine*, you know I am far from opposed to the idea that computers will one day achieve a kind of intelligence, albeit one alien to its inventors.

The trigger for this section, "Immutable Knowledge," was the idea of placing data and information into a database and somehow assuming that once captured and validated knowledge or information or data becomes immutable.

A credit bureau currently reports an incorrect address for me because a major department store told them I lived someplace other than where I live. My incorrect address at Camp Pendleton (I have no military history) remain immutable in the credit bureau's database. My only retort was a carefully worded note, of limited length, that documents my address history dispute.

That anecdote is data driven. Neither the system, nor the company that controls my records, displays any appreciable knowledge or wisdom. The data, once provided by a valid source, became immutable.

We are so concerned with gathering data and information that we forget we need time to digest what we read, to find connections between input and input, between what is known and what is new. If we learn only facts, then our knowledge becomes uninformed, our context obsolete. And our wisdom suffers the same fate, unable to determine what of our obsolete knowledge is best used to figure out the meaning of some new piece of data.

If I show my daughter Rachel a calculus book, she would have no context for understanding the symbols or the concepts. Rachel would reinvent the book based on her knowledge, creatively defining the symbols to mean things within her context of knowledge. A wonderful exercise in innovation, but not very fruitful in the search for knowledge representation or knowledge transfer.

I love my object-oriented database tools like Data Fellows' Vineyard and Xerox's Visual Recall. I can rapidly reflect my mind in an organic structure that facilitates personal organization and recall. The reflection, however, comes from my direct interaction. The application only facilitates building object structures, they do nothing to recommend organization beyond the basics such as last modification, document type, and name. Applications organize only the superficial.

To answer Eliot's questions, lost knowledge and wisdom reside in the potential of a million missed opportunities to consciously reflect, assimilate, and correlate our inputs. Objects store. We interpret. No matter the data repository, validity and meaning remain very human tasks. Perhaps this is the only immutable knowledge.

REVISITING METHODOLOGY

A methodology suggests a set of processes and norms which, when applied in a certain order with a certain rigor, produce a certain result. Methodologies suggest certainty. They suggest repeatability. As we know, however, in a world so riddled by uncertainty and chaos, that all a methodology can provide is guidance. Even the best execution of a project along a certain course will require innumerable small adjustments. Methodologies are abstractions of histories from one or many doing the same thing for a long period of time. They are generalities meant to mentor one along a river of thought. They are not meant as a finite map, but an aerial view. When the map fails and as chaos seems to encroach from all directions, everybody has to apply that skill almost certainly left out of the methodology guide, the skill we affectionately refer to as winging it.

The AI community has searched for rigorous processes that would transform a discipline comprised largely of knowledge representation built on individual biases to one of universal applicability. If we applied some process to knowledge, we would be able to build knowledge-based applications with the repetitiveness of an automobile driving off the production line in Detroit or Tokyo.

After years of effort, the grasping remains, but no methodology has asserted itself. The models of mind are too complex. No single representation suffices. Rules, genetic algorithms, and neural networks all require their own unique representations. And unlike traditional worlds dominated by standards like C, BASIC, and COBOL, no generalities can be made about the target code. The differences between inference engines and knowledge representations that seem so trivial on the surface, explode into a true semantic chaos in the details. In this case semantics is everything.

In addition to difficulties with tools and representations, we must also deal with the artifacts and the people. Unlike old IMS tables awaiting conversion into the more politically correct SQL, knowledge comes in many forms and shapes. Experts share no common parlance. Even on the same project, interviews and examples about the same task yield vastly different perspectives.

A method may help gather the knowledge consistently, but that is as far as it goes. The knowledge engineers must then reconcile multiple truths, even playing psychologist when they confront two revered experts with the real fact that, as experts neither their processes nor their results are the same. In the best scenarios, the experts open up to each other and learn. The expert system development project facilitates consensus and knowledge increases. In the worse case, the experts come to an impasse and the project fails for lack of a knowledge that can be codified.

KADS

But as guidance, methods have their place. They help organize and they help start projects. Although there is no unified methodology for AI work, Europe's ESPRIT funded project 1098 that led to the development of the Knowledge Acquisition and Structuring (KADS) methodology at the University of Amsterdam in 1983. KADS has now received further funding and is moving into its second phase as project P5248.

I like KADS. It is a methodology with a very broad aim, since it does contain knowledge in its moniker—it is, however, a methodology that knows its limits. KADS sees knowledge-based systems, not as repositories of human knowledge taken from an expert, but as an operational model. The development of knowledge-based systems is essentially modeling that reflects some behavior related to the real world.

KADS essentially uses available knowledge acquisition techniques to take concrete information about tasks, knowledge, and scenarios and create a conceptual model that houses the knowledge elements used by an expert, or experts, in solving a particular problem.

Beyond its very tight focus on the real world, KADS focuses on very specific problems. This helps reduce knowledge creep, the phenomenon that so often causes a small project to become a large project that never finishes because if the system doesn't understand the whole world, then it will make mistakes. Knowledge creep occurs when experts or knowledge engineers start incorporating knowledge on the edges of the domain into the system, which inches out the domain and adds the temptation to add just a little bit more to the new edges. Pretty soon those edges are pretty large and near impossible to manage.

Various implementations of KADS also include models of inference, tasks, and strategies. Inference models start with generic, domain-independent reasoning types, such as classification, diagnosis, and monitoring. It then maps high-level input-output knowledge elements, or metaclasses, through specific inference types.

Task models are expertise models that focus on detailed task descriptions derived from protocol analysis, task analysis, and scenario knowledge acquisition techniques. Finally, strategic models provide high-level representations of metaknowledge, describing the control and sequencing of inference and task components.

This stage generates a complete conceptual model that will provide a repository of knowledge that can then be structured into a particular tool. It also acts to focus discussions around elements described in terms that users and experts will understand. At this point the knowledge is represented in terms in which it was gathered.

As a KADS project progresses, it moves into physical implementation, testing, and other more mundane tasks. KADS does nothing to move from high-level concept to lower-level implementation, although some tools using the methodology's basic structure have been written for specific target systems. The plethora of knowledge systems and the lack of standards, however, make it impossible to generate code for any arbitrary target expert-system shell.

ESPRIT researchers found many holes in KADS-I that they hope to fill with KADS-II. They found the large granularity of models made it difficult to capture the fine grains of knowledge and process nuances associated with real-world knowledge systems. The very complexity of problem types brought them face-to-face with a problem OO folks know all too well: concept, object, and code management. When they started defining the wide variety of generic models, they soon found they were difficult to find when they needed them.

KADS is promising, but limited. Its value as a method derives from its developer's recognition of its limits. KADS focuses on productive uses of AI in areas where proven techniques work and avoids probing theoretical possibilities.

End PhaseKADS is a good attempt at bringing some level of order to the unorderly world of thought. KADS, like all AI projects, is a noble effort to help reduce the complexity of something very complex. In the mainframe days, we used to talk about the methodology religious wars, as IBM touted AD Cycle and James Martin pushed Information Engineering. Perhaps religion was an apt analogy, since one of its primary goals is to make the abstract and unknowable at least appear known and personal. There is comfort in process and ceremony.

As any Talmudic scholar or learned minister or priest will tell you, the more you know, the less you know. As they read the great commentaries of their religions, they find controversy and dissension, questions of faith, and even mistakes. Real life takes place in the details and it is far from perfect. The best a methodology can do is guide. The leaders on the edge will still wing it, no matter how hard we try to keep them to a path.

Human knowledge is a thing of great nuance. As I started researching for this section ("Revisiting Methodology") on the Web, I went to the only Web site that employs an ontologist. If anybody had bothered to classify knowledge acquisition and structuring, it would be Srinija Srinivasan, star classifier of Yahoo and former member of MCC's CYC project. I typed KADS into the search field in Yahoo and found out that KADS was not a methodology at all, but a radio station serving Elk City, Oklahoma. To be fair, KADS 1240 AM was not the only reference to KADS in the search—but Web searches, like a good methodology, prove that there are often no right answers, so the questions we ask may be more important than the results we achieve.

THE RULING CLASSES

Rules are the heart of knowledge-based systems. Yet despite the wide distribution of literature about rules and AI, most programmers see little difference between an IF ... THEN statement in C and one in an expert system shell. This section will point out those differences and discuss when rules are appropriate, even mandatory, to manage complex knowledge about business processes.

What Is a Rule?

A rule, in its raw state, is very similar to other IF ... THEN constructions found in programming languages as varied as HyperTalk and FORTRAN. The IF portion of a rule lists a number of conditions that must be met before the rule is considered true. The THEN portion of a rule lists several actions that take place when the rule is found TRUE. Some expert-system products include an ELSE clause, executed when the rule is found FALSE. In knowledge-based applications, the fact that a rule is FALSE is often as important as it is being TRUE.

Some rules accept only straight text or number relationships as conditions and conclusions. Other expert-system shells allow variables in both portions of the rule. These rules match patterns of attributes and values, making the rules more flexible and less numerous. By introducing pattern matching and variables, a single rule can represent a wide number of cases and states.

Rules are most often used to capture process-oriented knowledge. Rules represent processes as small declarative chunks. A rule does not incorporate all the conditions of a given process, but represents only a tractable portion of knowledge.

It is important that rules be small and self-contained. Rules with many conditions and actions can be difficult to debug and lead to a higher chance of conflict with other rules. Keeping the rule count between one to ten conditions provides some loose parameters. If you start getting beyond ten conditions, walk away from the rule and mull it over a bit. A rule with many conditions is probably an expedient way to enter knowledge, but it is hiding rules that you may need later for finer granularity in reasoning.

Before we leave Rules 101, it is important to remember that they are more than program constructs and more than logic. They represent human experience locked away in time. If you don't keep the human and the knowledge synchronized, the expert system logic will quickly wear into obsolescence. Rules remain an excellent way of capturing complex reasoning for software applications, but they require constant oversight and a lot of coddling.

Rule Reasoning

Rules are not much without a reasoning engine. With the exception of some generally available tools like OPS5 and CLIPS, written by universities or government agencies, most reasoning engines, and thus their knowledge representations, remain proprietary. The reasoning engine determines how rules look and how they behave. Rules differ from more common IF ... THEN constructions not so much on appearance, but on how they execute in memory. In a FORTRAN or C program, the decision construction of an IF ... THEN condition must be followed in sequence. Elaborate branching and nested conditions often make code unmanageable. Expert systems solve this problem by allowing rules to be entered and executed in any order.

One of the most common reasoning mechanisms is called *forward chaining*. In forward chaining data presented to the system causes rules to fire as the inference engine matches working memory data to rule conditions.

When all of a rule's conditions are met, a rule is said to be TRUE and its hypothesis is set to TRUE (some systems, like OPS5, rely strictly on the condition of data). The THEN portion of the rule is then evaluated, setting other variables to various values. All of this new data causes other rules to fire first, moving forward through chains of related rules.

Forward chaining is the best method to choose when the problem resolves into a large set of possible outcomes. The choice of many UNIX server options during the run of a configuration expert system would be a good example of forward chaining. Based on the customer's requirement for size, processor speed, memory, disk, and power, a large number of UNIX configurations are possible. Each set of requirements leads to a different conclusion.

Sometimes, however, a problem is tractable and can be decomposed into a well-described set of problems, subproblems, tasks, and subtasks. These problems are often characterized by representation in the form of a decision tree or decision table. Problems that fit in this category are best implemented using backward chaining.

In a backward-chained evaluation, the system is provided with something to prove. Most often this is done by suggesting or loading a particular hypothesis. The reasoning engine then fires rules that will confirm the state of the hypothesis. This is called backward chaining because a state graph of the process starts at a single point, commonly represented as a single hypothesis or goal, and expands backward through the rule base, matching goals and subgoals, until the state of the hypothesis is confirmed or denied.

Some systems combine forward and backward chaining into a "mixed mode" inference capability. Suggesting a goal may start backward chaining through the rule base, but as soon as sufficient data exists, the system starts looking for rules driven by the known data values for forward chaining.

It is perhaps at the end of a session that the expert system shows its biggest difference between rules and procedures. Or, I should say, at the end of a failed session. In standard languages, procedures always turn in a result. In an expert system the outcome of an inference sometimes meets a dead end. Because the knowledge is not infinite or even complete for its domain, expert systems often fail to resolve a question. Backward-chaining systems will either confirm or deny a suggested goal, but the reason for denial may be insufficient knowledge and does not necessary reflect the final answer on a given problem.

Rules and Objects

In most well-known commercial expert systems, rules interact with objects or frames. I will not go into the difference between these two again; you can read previous sections to see those distinctions. Since we are concentrating here on rules, the difference is non-existent for practical purposes. Rules reason about things, and in modern expert system products, those things are represented by frames and objects.

Objects have attributes, and the values assigned to those attributes become the driving force in data-driven systems. In systems like Neuron Data's Nexpert Object, everything, with the exception of the rules themselves, are objects. A hypothesis is a Boolean object-attribute pair. It need not be an isolated object. I usually assign the attribute as object_name.*hypo* where *hypo* is a Boolean attribute.

The object object_name may have other attributes for storing text, numbers, or other Boolean values.

As an inference session initiates, several values are set to their defaults, or assigned values via the user interface. Most commercial tools tightly combine the graphical user interface and the rule/object structures. In some systems the objects for GUI widgets are just objects off another branch of the object hierarchy. In others the GUI objects are separate from the objects being reasoned over.

In either case, the reasoning engine requires answers to questions. Objects act as the interface points between rules and the needed data. The IF-NEEDED slot executes to define how the object is to receive its value. The value can come from a variety of sources, including SQL tables, direct questions through the interface, inheritance down the object structure, implementation of default values, and so forth. In many expert systems a series of these sources can be listed. The inference engine will travel through the source list until an unambiguous answer is instantiated.

Rules and objects make ideal companions. Rules alone can create knowledge bases of high sophistication. In corporate environments, however, modern expert systems that combine objects and rules, along with graphical user interface tools, make for more robust, more understandable, and easier-to-maintain systems.

When to Rule

Deciding when to use rules is really a decision as to when AI techniques should be introduced into software applications. My rule of thumb comes down to complexity. When the knowledge in the system, in the form of conditional statements, reaches a point at which it is unmanageable by an average programmer, then an expert system solution is in order. Of course it is better to be proactive, and the amount of knowledge in a system is better identified during the analysis phase.

The introduction of rules and inferencing into an application can lead to significant increases in development time. As I have discussed in these pages before, knowledge acquisition, verification and testing make already complicated applications very complicated. Systems analysis is not enough. You will need knowledge engineering, and once you begin to embed knowledge into applications, you will have to maintain a staff of knowledge engineers or keep around the phone numbers for good knowledge engineering consultants.

As the business changes the knowledge about the business will have to be adapted. Rules provide a flexible place to maintain knowledge without the complete restructuring of applications. Separating rules from primary logic requires excellent design and programming skills. The process of decoupling logic and knowledge takes longer, but the payoff is a solid application with a flexible knowledge base that can grow and change as the business evolves.

End State

Rule-based systems are best combined with objects to provide rich environments for capturing knowledge. No single knowledge representation scheme is sufficient for all types of knowledge. Most expert-system products combine rules and objects, along with demons, to allow for complex relationships and actions. Along with these knowledge representation methods come a variety of reasoning mechanisms for evaluating the state of rules and frames.

At the heart of AI is the rule. It is also its most severe constraint. The early expert system MYCIN established rules as primary for logic representation in expert systems. As we delve more into the mind, we find that our brains are far from being simple logic engines driven by rules. Each generation of research leads to new ways of mimicking our human capabilities.

For now, rules and frames represent the majority of expert-system programming tools on the market—and these tools are important components of software engineering tool chests. Knowing when to employ rules and being patient enough to gather the knowledge and represent it properly can lead to dramatic new applications of software for process evaluation, monitoring, and assistance.

APIs to expert-system shells and knowledge-based class libraries present excellent, cost-effective ways to incorporate knowledge into a system. Even if you only start small, adding knowledge to a system can increase its robustness for solving problems. Once the rule-base is incorporated, the application can be changed by modifying rules, not the internals of the application. And because rules are easier to understand than traditional procedural code, customers can participate more in their development and maintenance.

Rules are the heart of knowledge-based systems. Many application programs, written in a variety of languages, would benefit from knowledge-based approaches to data management and diagnosis. Many business problems are suitable for knowledge-based solutions. For the 1990s and beyond, a good understanding of rules and inference will make you a better programmer, and your systems more adaptable to the daily changes of the business. world.

NOTE

1. I use structure English here rather than any particular shell syntax.

4

AI APPLICATIONS

The use of AI is widespread though difficult to document with specifics. Most organizations are leery of disclosing information about technology advantages in competitive markets. The abundance of AI applications, however, will become apparent as I describe over a dozen applications from major corporations and government agencies.

OBJECTS AND AI APPLICATIONS

First, I am going to start with the system I know best: The Surface Mount Assembly Reasoning Tool (SMART) developed at Western Digital in the mid-1980s. Although I have developed other systems since SMART, no other system brought to me the wealth of learning associated with SMART. I hope the story proves at least a fraction as valuable as I found the actual experience.

Getting SMART

When I first thought about applying AI to manufacturing, the choices of applications seemed overwhelming. Many challenges faced Western Digital as it implemented new technologies related to mounting resistors and integrated circuits directly onto the surface of a printed circuit board. Only a dollop of solder separated the component from the board. As the manufacturing engineers struggled to perfect the mix of heat, solder, components, and processes, they discovered an interesting phenomenon. Things had to be manufactured. It was no longer sufficient to engineer solutions, the engineers were needed to write the programs that drove the factory.

And as the product mix increased, the time engineers were able to spend perfecting their processes decreased. They had to go with what they had; the pressures of the market called for good product, not necessarily perfect processes or the best technology. Besides, switching to the latest technology meant spending money, and the current surface mount equipment worked. They had to concentrate on keeping up with the ever-expanding product line and figure out how to make it better later.

The manufacturing engineering ranks soon grew frustrated. They were hired to implement the latest and best manufacturing technology, and they were responsible not for maintaining it, but improving it. Almost seventy-five percent of their time was now spent writing and perfecting programs for the existing production line. That was when I joined the team as the manager of computer-assisted manufacturing. My responsibility included automating human processes, relieving the manufacturing engineers of mental grunt work that led to their frustration, and support the staff with software that would allow them to achieve their goals.

At the first staff meeting I shared my list of ideas and said that none of them looked like the solution to their frustration. At that point I turned to the manufacturing engineering manager and asked him what pissed him off. And in the context of software and programming, he shared the situation I outlined above. He talked about his team's desire to contribute to the bottom line by implementing the best manufacturing technology, but that they were now concentrating most of their time on writing programs for the existing manufacturing line, knowing all the time their cutting edge skills were slowly being shaved back by the sharp edge of real production.

Within a few days I outlined the plans for SMART, the Surface Mount Assembly Reasoning Tool. A few weeks later the funding for the project arrived in my budget. It was time to start.

It was decided that the kind of expertise required to build SMART would be difficult to justify as permanent staff positions, so we immediately started searching for a competent consulting firm interested in Western Digital, manufacturing, and writing innovative software, even if that software was on a shoestring budget. The use of a consulting firm provided important elements to the overall expert-system development effort. After a five-day trip through Silicon Valley, the mecca of AI in the 1980s, both the tool and the consulting firm were chosen. We would code the system in Nexpert Object and work with Bechtel AI Institute.

The choice of tool was fairly easy. I was a Nexpert programmer, so we were predisposed to Neuron Data's product. Bechtel was a surprise, however, as a contractor. Many of the other firms certainly displayed competence, but they did so coolly and with an aloofness I did not feel would meld well with Western Digital's somewhat more earthy culture. We flew by the seat of our pants in a rapidly changing market. Products came and went in cycles as short as six months. There was no time to delve into the academic significance of the effort, we needed practical results to help our growing business keep up with the pace of change.

Bechtel displayed an almost child-like enthusiasm for process. They thought what we were doing was "neat." The brief meeting near the Bechtel boardroom convinced us almost immediately that we had found our team. Within a few weeks we inked the deal and started work. Bechtel provided software engineers, knowledge engineers, and project managers. The project was staffed and ready to go.

As we continued through the process, the requirements for SMART became clearer. The work of the manufacturing engineer also included knowledge about which machine to place which components on, when several machines could do the job, and how to balance the load across machines so that no single machine paced the line. The task went from the macro of choosing the right machines and the right order of components, to the micro of how to maximize the placement of components on an individual machine.

Doubts and Design

Some people at Western Digital believed that AI was the wrong choice. They believed that the primary idea behind line balancing would prove to be statistical in nature and AI would only complicate the tasks. But, as we built the RFQ, we found that there were several available heuristics that would not easily translate to C or Pascal.

With a few presentations of the nature of the problem, the algorithmic opponents slipped into the background.

The first SMART phased project plan consisted of several milestones:

- ☑ Create a component level manufacturing database with information pertinent to the SMART program.

- ☑ Demonstrate a prototype on a known board type and a single pick and place machine.

- ☑ Deliver a production prototype that could program any machine in any factory.

- ☑ Refine the system and install it in factories.

Except for starts and stops caused by the tightening or loosening of corporate purse strings, the project proceeded punctually and achieved the technical goals set out for each section of the project. As the project progressed, focus changed from the expert-system technology, which was proving itself through testing trials, to the in-house difficulties of linking diverse systems.

The database used early in the project was hand-keyed because no corporate database existed that would link CAD, manufacturing, and manufacturing engineering data. Toward the end of the production prototype phase, design automation created a series of programs that would link this data. As we received the information for SMART trials, we realized the difficulty in getting consistent information from systems that were updated in real time at different stations and at different times. We rarely found a trouble-free data set that worked without modification. We developed a corporate repository that synchronized all the information prior to entering it into SMART. This database not only aided the manufacturing engineers through SMART, but proved valuable for eliminating duplicate component specifications, reducing overall costs to the operation.

The Benefits of SMART

SMART was conceived as a way to eliminate the need for manufacturing engineers to program pick-and-place machines "long hand."

But, as we explored the benefits of such a system, we realized the benefits greatly surpassed labor savings alone.

Short-Term Benefits

The short-term benefits of SMART included the following:

☑ **An optimum program instead of a prototype program—** In some situations, manufacturing engineers do not have time to write good programs. SMART would allow them to write good programs every time.

☑ **A reduced design-to-production cycle time for Surface Mount Technology boards—**Since the manual method required about one week of elapsed time to complete an efficient program, SMART shortened cycle time, and time to market, by one week.

☑ **Written programs that were optimized for a given line configuration—**Novice programmers often wrote inefficient programs that did not run the production line at maximum throughput. These programs may have inefficient pick-and-place sequences or unbalanced line configurations. The use of SMART eliminated this condition and the output acted as a coach to novice programmers so they could learn what good programs looked like.

☑ **The improved ability to react to customer demands and environmental changes—**Because SMART can write programs quickly, using it allowed Western Digital to create new programs for board configuration changes driven by last minute customer requests.

☑ **A more accurate program from elimination of data transcription error—**In the long-hand method, transcription errors were often encountered. "Clean data" in SMART eliminated this problem.

☑ **A reduced need to hire additional manufacturing engineering staff for programming—**The use of SMART minimized the need to hire new manufacturing engineering staff to support programming.

☑ **Reduced information research**—SMART used an integrated manufacturing database for input, eliminating the need for the manufacturing engineers to research a part's manufacturing information.

☑ **Reduced paperwork**—SMART generated all reports required to support manufacturing engineering deliverables such as load sheets, program sheets, and so forth.

☑ **Reduced routine efforts**—Manufacturing engineers who use SMART can invest more of their time in problem-solving endeavors, rather than the mundane programming they have already mastered.

Long-Term Benefits

SMART's long-term benefits included the following abilities to:

☑ **Provide factory flexibility during a down machine condition**—If a machine goes down, SMART could rewrite programs to work around down machines, generating a best-fit program given remaining machines.

☑ **Compare alternative courses of action**—SMART evaluated production lines and helped determine which line scenario was best for new products. Alternately, SMART could test the efficiency of new lines by using its knowledge of existing machines placed in new configurations.

☑ **Write routings for use in Western Digital's central manufacturing system**—Because SMART knows the timing on the pick-and-place machine, a future enhancement could allow it to determine the complete routing sequence for a given board and provide that information to the enterprise manufacturing system.

☑ **Be used to feed an electronic documentation system—** SMART output is completely electronic. If Western Digital chooses to develop a centralized electronic storage system, SMART programs could be stored in it for easy retrieval.

☑ **Develop standard cost models for products—**If SMART knows timings and routings, cost information could be included for standard cost model development.

Many of the long-term benefits predicted for SMART never materialized. It paid for itself with the early benefits, and although successful, my leaving Western Digital left SMART without a vocal sponsor. Although SMART was polished up and ran for several years after I left, the final set of tasks were never implemented.

Technically Speaking ...

Technically, planning the assembly of the surface mount components on a board consists of two main tasks:

☑ Assigning to each SMT machine on the assembly line the components that it should place (line balancing).

☑ Determining the placement sequence (the program) for the components on each machine.

Each of these tasks was implemented in a separate phase of SMART. During the first phase, we built a system to determine the placement sequence for small boards built by one machine. During the second, we extended this system to include line balancing for assembly lines with multiple machines and a greater variety of boards.

Before SMART, line balancing and program generation were done by manufacturing engineers, who had developed a set of techniques—heuristics—for accomplishing these tasks. In a series of knowledge acquisition sessions, two knowledge engineers worked to elicit these techniques, with the goal of reproducing them as the expert system. We found direct representation to be possible for some heuristics, but some engineers' decisions made use of extensive information, including visual information, and were of a complexity beyond the scope of our system. For such decisions, we tried to preserve the spirit of their approach using, where appropriate, a mathematical technique to approximate it.

One example is the grouping of components of the same part type. The components of a PCB—transistors, resistors, and so on—come packaged on reels of tape; each reel carries components of a single part type. These reels are loaded on a cassette drive on the machine, and the drive has a limited number of reel positions. In addition, the shop may stock a limited number of reels for a given part. For these reasons, the engineers attempt to minimize the number of reels by sequentially loading components of the same part type. They balance the requirement to minimize the distance between sequential components against the requirement to minimize the number of reels.

We did not feel we could directly capture all the information and reasoning involved in decisions of this type, and instead, implemented what seemed to us to be the key process, namely, grouping components of the same part type by location. We used statistical algorithms to identify geometric groupings of components of the same type. The combination of direct representation of expert heuristics, where possible, and approximate representation using, where appropriate, mathematical algorithms, was our general approach in building SMART.

In determining the sequence of components, the engineer takes several considerations into account. The main goal is to minimize time needed to place all components, while also satisfying other constraints—specifically, the previously mentioned need to minimize the number of reels. Contributing to the amount of time are the:

- Distance between sequentially placed components.

- Speed at which parts of the machine can operate while placing specific components.

- Use of certain machine facilities.

Distance has an obvious relation to placement time; placement time will increase as the distance from the previous component increases. In addition, some systems on the machine operate more slowly for heavier components. Components placed immediately before it will also use the slower speed. Finally, certain machine facilities are mechanically paired, and a certain period of time must elapse after the first facility has been used before its partner is available for use.

These three factors, and the requirement to minimize reels, are often at odds with one another, and the engineer uses different techniques to balance them. We abstracted these techniques into several heuristics:

☑ Statistically identify components of the same part type to be loaded from one reel.

☑ Group components by placement speed and use of critical machine facilities.

☑ Identify a path to be followed based on board geometry.

☑ Place each group of components. The criteria used in choosing the next component within a group include the direction of movement and distance from the previous placed component.

Line Balancing

Normally, an SMT assembly line consists of three or four machines, each of which is capable of placing different part types. Sometimes, two machines of the same type may exist on one line, and in any event, normally, many components can be placed by more than one machine on the line. In such a case, the goal of line balancing is to distribute the components so a minimum cycle time can be achieved. There are essentially two parts to this task:

☑ Identify the number of components to be placed by each machine.

☑ Identify which specific components will be placed by each machine.

For those components that could be placed by more than one machine on the line, the engineers use mathematical equations to determine the number to place on each machine. These equations incorporate the manufacturer's estimate of time to place components of a specific part type. SMART implements this process with standard linear programming algorithms.

In determining where specific components should be placed, SMART follows the engineers' preference for assigning components to a contiguous area on the board. SMART divides the board such that the computed number of components can be assigned to each machine.

Implementation Issues

SMART is written in Nexpert Object and C and runs under Windows. Nexpert Object was a good choice for development because of its system integration facilities and its expert-system features. Nexpert's open architecture has enabled us to:

- ☑ Build a user interface using the full range of WINDOWS facilities.

- ☑ Use a commercial database management system to produce system reports.

- ☑ Write computationally intensive processes in C, and access these routines from the knowledge base.

Nexpert's object-oriented facilities provided an intuitive way to represent the problem domain—the board, the machines, the components, and so forth—and this was valuable during early system development, and even more valuable during system expansion.

Nexpert rules represent all non-computationally intense reasoning and also handled the flow of control for the entire application.

Lessons Learned

The initial project was delivered in April of 1989 and was modified to include line balancing in September of 1989. The most recent deliveries included refinements to the line balancing knowledge, an improved user interface, and post-editing capabilities for the program data so manufacturing engineers can fix the information when

SMART does a less than perfect (or preferred) job. By including the post-editing capability, SMART evolved from an independent black-box to a manufacturing engineering partner.

Along the development path we learned several things about software development, user relations, and corporate databases. In the software arena we learned that preliminary designs can be close to reality if they are thoroughly discussed and specified, but even close designs need modification in practice. A flow chart of SMART done early in the process is almost identical to one that would be drawn today, but beneath the major modules, infinitesimal design changes and major interface modifications have taken the program beyond its original description. We found that different board types required different strategies in the system. In the early days a board was a board. We discovered that manufacturing engineers want to interact with the system, not just get output. In the early days we were designing a black box.

SMART has forced Western Digital to examine and redefine its information strategy for manufacturing information. Groups that once worked independently are now working in unison to solve data compatibility problems. SMART has also caused manufacturing engineers to reexamine their requirements and their thought processes. Early speculation leaned toward the tool making programmers less efficient, but we are finding that the system is making them better programmers as they attack faults in SMART's reasoning model. Both SMART and the engineering staff benefit from such interactions.

SMART was eventually implemented at several Western Digital sites worldwide. Prior to a change at Western Digital that drove product strategies toward drives and away from board manufacturing, SMART proved a reliable supplement to scarce manufacturing knowledge. SMART's success is just one story of a successful melding of knowledge and objects. The next section of this chapter covers many other applications of object and AI.

OTHER APPLICATIONS OF AI AND OBJECTS

I have talked about SMART several times over the years, but the story above gives a pretty good chronicle of the effort. SMART, however, is not the only expert system ever written. AI technology plays a major role today in everything from Wizards in Microsoft Office to analyzing input about insurance claims or finance applications. The rambling exploration that follows provides a perspective on the applications of AI to business problems.

- ☑ At Fannie Mae, the Desktop Underwriter processes 25,000 loan applications per month, reducing the cost of manual underwriting for the nations mortgage lenders and for Fannie Mae.

- ☑ At MetLife, the MetLife Intelligent Text Analyzer extracts information from free-form fields on insurance applications and categorizes the information for underwriters.

- ☑ The Provider Selection Tool at Oxford Health Plan, Inc. works interactively with call center personnel to help new clients choose their right kinds of plans based on their personal profiles.

- ☑ The Integrated Diagnostic System at the National Research Council of Canada helps diagnose problems and suggests repair processes for commercial aircraft fleets.

- ☑ Union Pacific Railroad uses its Rail Train Scheduler to generate schedules and allocate resources for the replacement of over 31,000 miles of track over a twenty-four state region. This single application will save Union Pacific about half a million dollars a year.

These are not historical expert systems, derived from researching several antique books about the early days of AI. You see no reference here to MYCIN or STRIPS. These applications all won awards in 1997, and they were all implemented with ART*Enterprise from Brightware, Inc.

But other companies have their stories as well. Neuron Data's Elements Expert (formerly Nexpert Object) helped American Greetings manage its business, which generates more than 20,000 new designs a year and ships over 2.4 billion cards. Elements Expert helped American Greetings transform an old job shop mentality into a modern cellular manufacturing facility, with Elements Expert orchestrating the planning and execution of factory work. Lead times have dwindled from 21 weeks to 7. Finished inventory was cut by $22 and lot sizes have gone from 60,000 to 30,000.

Sometimes expertise is best brought in from scratch using one of the oldest and most successful languages in computer science, LISP. LISP was the language of AI for many years, before the basic capabilities of rules and frames migrated to C or C++. But as software clay, nothing works better than LISP in helping programmers explore concepts and literally see their ideas work as quickly as they enter them.

Price Waterhouse used Allegro Common LISP to create the Audit Expert System, which assists accounting professions in choosing audit procedures given a particular company's profile. Jeff Delisio, Research Scientist at Price Waterhouse's Technology Center said, "Using Allegro CL and CLOS, we were able to quickly change the underlying structure of our program to reflect input from our knowledge experts, and reduce the time required to deploy the application." Price Waterhouse also used LISP to create their Modeling and Analysis System, which helps model and analyze business processes for building hierarchical, structured textually annotated flowcharts that reflect client business processes and internal controls.

Crash Bandicoot Naughty Dog Software also liked LISP so much that the Universal City, California company used it to develop Crash Bandicoot, a game title for the Sony Playstation. Naughty Dog used Allegro CL for the character control portions of the game. The character control and AI written in LISP enabled the development of over 500 different types of game objects, each with uniquely crafted and tuned game play and visual characteristics.

According to Naughty Dog cofounder Andy Gavin, the unique capabilities of Allegro CL's LISP language enabled very fast development and execution of character and object control. Crash is filled with all sorts of creatures and devices constructed in full 3-D and interacting with the player in real time (30 frames per second).

"LISP was just the best solution for this job," comments Gavin. "With leading-edge game systems like ours, you have to deal with complicated behaviors and real-time action. Languages like C are very poor with temporal constructs. C is just very awkward for a project like this. LISP, on the other hand, is ideal."

As Gavin explains, "With LISP one can rapidly develop metaconstructs for behaviors and combine them in new ways. In addition, LISP allows the redefinition of the language to easily add new constructs, particularly those needed to deal with time-based behaviors and the layering of actions. Contrary to popular belief there is nothing inherently slow about LISP. It is easy to construct a simple dialect which is just as efficient as C, but retains the dynamic and consistent qualities that make LISP a much more effective expression of one's programming intentions."

For the Crash Bandicoot project, Naughty Dog used Allegro CL to create a programming language called GOOL (Game Object-Oriented Language), which is specifically geared to game development. Using this Allegro CL-based language, the team was able to produce hundreds of different game objects with sophisticated real-time behavior and animation. These behaviors are faster to develop, and more compact than an equivalent C program, allowing for rapid prototyping and experimentation. The result, says Gavin, is "we've got the hottest, most highly regarded new game on the major gaming platform of the moment."

There are hundreds of applications that prove AI's value to business, even if they are the hottest or most highly regarded. Smart objects help major corporations achieve their goals, leveraging the knowledge of experienced workers while maintaining quality and lower costs. If you have any questions about using AI technology, ask them yourself.

Perhaps my best advice is to use these tools with a minimum of publicity. They cost no more than other tools these days and run on standard hardware. Use them, but do not bring the raging light of management scrutiny to your smart object applications any more than you would an Oracle application. You don't ask the president of the company when you use C over COBOL; why ask if you use C++ or an expert-system shell? Perhaps the level of skill required to bring a project to fruition will be slightly more, and perhaps the human experts in the project will need to divulge more of their knowledge, but these are both good things. As organizations move toward the area of knowledge management, they need to become more reflective and more prepared to share.

So look to IBM's Product Cost Estimator or Canon's Strategic Account Management System for inspiration. Look to Ford's Computer Aided Parts Estimation too or Kraft's Problem Solving System for Kraft Pulp Mills. Your problems and your expertise are unique, but many have paved the cow paths and plowed the road before you. Take these stories to heart and realize that even if the esoteric philosophy found elsewhere in this book doesn't inspire corporate confidence in smart objects, that these stories of systems in everyday use in major corporations will help you see that software has not yet started to make its contribution to the bottom line.

As most and more expert systems find their way into major corporations, we may finally see what Ed Feigenbaum terms the "rise of the expert company" as he speculated on these same ideas over ten years ago in his book by that name.

THE OBJECT OF MANUFACTURING

In the late '70s and early '80s Computer Integrated Manufacturing (CIM) was all the rage. System vendors from IBM to DEC to Burroughs tried to sell their customers fully integrated manufacturing visions that tied the shop floor to the material plan, and the material plan to accounts payable.

Manufacturing Resource Planning (MRP II) and its connection to the factory floor became a software silver bullet. Because of its reliance on monolithic, proprietary architectures, the CIM silver bullet failed to strike its target. Objects, with their ability to communicate across a network and capture the essence of complex physical things, may offer the CIM silver bullet a new chance to outrun the superman of probability.

A Manufacturing History Lesson

MRP II takes sales orders and forecasts as input and generates detailed plans for the parts and machines that will create them; extrapolations from this data provide cash flow and other financial forecasts. The number of manufacturing companies that successfully implemented Manufacturing Resource Planning (MRP II), from the return on investment point of view, remains small. Many companies use pieces of MRP, but few have achieved its promise.

CIM attempted to extend MRP's reach to the factory floor. CIM was to extend MRP's plans to execution. CIM required an integrated factory floor where controllers on machines received instruction and returned results to a central computer, which in turn, fed actual data into MRP.

The integration of the business applications was successful from the technical point of view. The large databases and tons of COBOL that comprise MRP always run well in data processing. Integrating

MRP with proprietary factory systems proves difficult. And without a realistic link to the factory, savvy managers will find excuses to disregard the system.

To combat the integration problem, large vendors proposed standards. Unfortunately, these standards were as proprietary as the hodgepodge of systems already in the factory. The vendor's argument is at least there is only one. However, that one set of standards still required thousands of programming hours to integrate mainframe computers or minicomputers and programmable logic controllers from dozens of vendors. Often the only thing these boxes had in common was a power cord and an RS-232 port.

The business systems integrated, but most factories were ill-equipped to invest in writing their own code to link their sea of point solutions. Objects proved a new alternative.

The Object Impact

CIM's Achilles' heel was shop floor integration. Long, in-house developed applications that translated data from mainframe to factory controller proved expensive and hard to maintain. Objects, open systems, and standard, low cost hardware change the equation. Personal computers and workstations are pushing out proprietary shop floor computers. The long lines of monolithic code are giving way to processes understood and decomposed into process diagrams. Objects will provide the foundation for interoperable, modular, interchangeable, and integrated software. With standards like CORBA, hardware vendors will soon be able to create to factory- and enterprise-level object interfaces.

The impact of objects, however, goes beyond the technical ability to communicate with hardware. Manufacturing people are pragmatic and visual. They sense off-key grinding noises behind veils of oily vapor, they see fractionally skewed chips on printed circuit boards, and they find burrs on paper-thin sheet metal. Computers have always been intruders in the factory. Forepersons and line workers must see a reason to change their way of doing business.

Intelligent machines and computer assisted manufacturing programs are removing the burden of learning numerical control programming. Object-oriented graphical interfaces are transforming dull character-based terminals into useful, visually striking tools for tracking work and planning the future. The desktop metaphor blends easily with the clutter of sheet metal calendars and Caterpillar baseball caps.

I remember my Dad sitting at a teletype machine, with calculator in hand, punching paper tape programs for an automatic punch press. It took several hours to create a program for a single battery charger cover. Today a computer assisted manufacturing program reads an IGES file and provides the tape. Dad always found programming a challenge, but never really liked it. With object representations of a sheet cover, the design will automatically change the program with each engineering iteration. The program will be a by-product of the process.

The Representation of Things

To integrate process and product requires a robust model for data. Relational, hierarchical, and network database managers are excellent for storing the abstract, made up data of business data processing. But manufacturing is a tangible world. Things are made of things and by things. Things transform things and communicate with things. Objects are the best information science answer to the capture and retention of things. Objects capture the relationships and subtleties of parent component relationships, machine behaviors, and version upon version of engineering documentation. Objects snare the manufacturing world in one multisensory gulp.

Relational databases and SQL may help integrate manufacturing planning, cost, and other business data, but they will do little to integrate manufacturing and engineering. Even more than manufacturing, engineering deals with things. It deals with CAD drawings and material specifications; it deals with versions of documents. The bill of material and part master records at the heart of manufacturing systems fail to capture the mounds of part description data stored in file cabinets and engineering lockers.

Imagine a printed circuit board viewed in color bitmap mode. Conventional technology requires imports and exports between divergent data models. Applications read the exported data and analyze it—the analysis, however, is connected only tangentially (through the exported data) to its original representation. With an object representation it will be able to produce simulation results, display the part's CAD image, or provide quality information because the underlying model remains intact.

The US and foreign governments are looking for standards that will create robust information models that integrate companies and industries. For military contracts the US Government initiated the Computer Aided Logistics System (CALS) initiative. CALS is working toward a unification of engineering and manufacturing data through the Product Data Exchange using STEP (PDES) and the Standard for Exchange of Product Model Data (STEP), two interrelated standards for representing the details of components and assemblies. Several companies, including Auto-trol Technology, DEC, and IBM have working PDES-compliant databases.

Auto-trol built its STEP-based Mozaic architecture on the Object Store object-oriented database from Object Design. They are now working with several vendors to create versions of CAD/CAM tools that will work within the Mozaic framework. All the products will exchange data through a single data model that is independent of the database, the hardware platform, or the other cooperating applications. Mozaic represents one of the first manufacturing applications to take advantage of the modularity and platform independence that comes from object-oriented technologies.

As PDES-compliant products evolve, they will save their data in PDES format. Unlike the initial graphics exchange standard (IGES), PDES captures much more than two- and three-dimensional geometries. PDES is capable of capturing stress, thermal, and inventory information. Currently, engineering organizations must write or buy translators for the import/export of IGES or proprietary files to specialized CAD/CAE systems like thermal analysis programs. With a PDES-compliant database, the drafting program would save 3-D data to PDES attributes. The thermal program would read the 3-D data, execute its analysis, and then populate related attributes with the results.

PDES was not intended for object-oriented databases. Implementors, however, found objects the most natural fit for the new standard. Eventually the power of objects will directly influence standards. Objects allow for concurrent views of a single object. A printed circuit board, for instance, can be viewed as an assembly, as a schema, or as colored dots on a warehouse map that shows the relationship between the board components and their inventory locations. This can all be accomplished with a single representation of a board interacting with other object representations throughout the enterprise.

The Object of Application

Very few applications of objects to manufacturing exist in established manufacturing firms. Corporate and university laboratories are examining objects for experimental and commercial projects. Many of these projects include intelligent objects called agents.

Agents derive from the discipline of Distributed Artificial Intelligence that explores interaction models for societies of intelligent agents. Intelligent agents in manufacturing applications negotiate deals and come to find consensus designs, generate schedules, and manage resources.

In May of 1992, the University of Calgary sponsored the International Conference on Object-Oriented Manufacturing Systems (ICOOMS) in Calgary, Alberta (Canada). Over fifty conference papers covered the promise and future of object applications in manufacturing. Running through all of the papers was a central theme of object representation. Objects capture parent component relationships and document relationships, versions, and the sequence of steps used to contort raw sheet metal into an automobile fender.

The researchers and members of industry that presented at ICOOMS found applications for objects in concurrent engineering, product modeling, feature-based design, factory control systems, production planning and control, enterprise modeling, scheduling, modeling and simulation, layout and maintenance, assembly, and flexible manufacturing.

At the Society of Manufacturing Engineers' annual AUTOFACT November gathering in Detroit, objects permeated the show. Small vendors, like STEP Tools Inc., showed tools for supporting the implementation of STEP (PDES) in CAD/CAM and CAE applications. Large vendors, like ComputerVision (Bedford, MA) and Wisdom Systems (Pepper Pike, OH) discussed or demonstrated object-oriented futures for the CAD systems.

In Palo Alto, California, Stanford University researchers formed Enterprise Integration Technologies to create an object-oriented factory control system for the fabrication of integrated circuits. The Manufacturing Knowledge Systems (MKS) and its object-oriented database integrate applications ranging from simulation to scheduling and process engineering to process diagnosis. MKS strives to capture the data and knowledge that integrate an entire enterprise. MKS also employs intelligent agents to solve practical problems like monitoring processes, equipment, and materials.

Objects are coming. They will first be felt under the darkened lights of the CAD rooms and then by the rest of the engineering community. Within the next few years objects will invade the manufacturing floor, providing access to engineering drawings and simulations, work instructions, and warning us when the factory is out of control.

Problems Remain

Standards for objects continue to be sparse and incomplete. The Object Management Group's Common Object Request Broker Architecture (CORBA) helps detail object interactions, but it does not specify internal syntax and semantics. Manufacturers tend to be conservative. Relational databases and the clear similarities between implementations provide comfort even for managers without technical backgrounds.

Objects do not currently provide the same level of comfort. Objects are clearly easier to understand because of their similarities to manufacturing representations of assemblies and components. Message passing, encapsulation, and polymorphism are technical terms still used too often in the presence of the uninitiated. When was the last time you heard an Oracle salesman discuss Cartesian set theory?

For objects to be accepted they must be *businessized*. Standards will help information professionals feel comfortable. The managers and end users must begin hearing about business solutions, not technology. SQL only became popular when it saved costs and supported business needs like distributed decision support.

Hearing No Objections

We are moving toward an organic metaphor for computers. Manufacturing has always understood the relevance of nature to the human process. Manufacturing is the saga of state transitions from one thing to another. Iron ore smelts to hardened steel and beach sand seizes the finely etched circuits of a computer chip.

Shrinking investments in manufacturing may leave companies unable to leverage the potential of objects. The cost will be high. The object of this lesson is finding the courage to change.

WHERE AI MEETS THE SHOP FLOOR

*If we value the pursuit of knowledge, we must be free to
follow wherever that search may lead us. The free mind is
no barking dog, to be tethered on a ten-foot chain.*
                    —Adlai Stevenson,
                        University of Wisconsin, October 8, 1952

Trying to build the ultimate shop floor scheduling application as
your first AI attempt will turn you toward the crowd face down
much like a gymnast who overextends her talents. Previously we
talked about starting small. We talked about tools that buffered you
from much of the AI experience and placed you in the manufacturing domain where you could finish with both feet planted firmly
in the ground. But AI is many things beside diagnostic expert systems
and shop floor schedulers. Over the years I have developed several
intelligent shop documentation systems that combine AI technology
with hypertext. These text and graphic presentation systems may not
be as sexy as XCON or DISPATCHER, but they are practical, non-
trivial applications you can develop in-house. Before you start your
Olympic AI career, make sure you win a few local matches to build
your confidence and the confidence of your sponsors.

Reading Between the Lines

Almost everyone in manufacturing edited, read, or disregarded manufacturing standards manuals or workmanship standards manuals.
These books are often wonderful tools for helping a manufacturing
engineer fulfill his or her management by objective (MBO) tasks, but
they are poor tools for people on the shop floor.

Most of these manuals consist of very structured words for communicating how things should be done in an ideal factory. Many of
them even contain hints about what should be done if things go
awry, but the information contained in these books is often difficult
to read and even more difficult to find. If you are working on a manufacturing line and all of a sudden the conveyor belt starts dropping
printed circuit boards on the floor, where are you going to look for
help? Nine times out of ten you are probably going to call for a manufacturing engineer. The last thing you are going to do is consult
a manual.

If much of what your manufacturing engineer knew about fixing conveyor belts was captured in an intelligent documentation system, you could consult a terminal faster than you could scream for help.

Writing Down the Tasks

Finding the right application is the first and most important element in developing an intelligent documentation system. Look through the list of applications in the sidebar, "Application Ideas" for inspiration. Anything that is currently found in notebooks or on cheat sheets is a prime candidate.

APPLICATIONS IDEAS

Diagnostic and Repair Systems. Because these systems are often decision tree based, the decision nodes can be coded into hypertext systems much like they would be in a system like Texas Instrument's Procedure Consultant.

Preventative Maintenance. These systems are close cousins to diagnostic and repair manuals, but they are designed to anticipate problems so their structure must be more procedural on the front end. Their intelligence comes in after a problem is found.

Assembly Aids. By putting your assembly documentation into an intelligent system, operators could scan a bar code and the system would display the appropriate assembly information.

Company Policy. The shop floor is often a scene of employee dissatisfaction. When there is no controversy, there are often questions. By putting your personnel and financial policies into intelligent systems you could eliminate many calls to finance and human resources.

Engineering Procedures. Documents like ECO control and implementation, new part releases, and engineering change requests could be placed into hypertext systems.

Think about the things that people refer to, scraps of paper that have no purpose except to aid in a portion of some manufacturing task. How about incoming inspection instructions, security procedures, even the company newsletter? Brainstorm a few ideas and look for one where you know the department would cooperate. Believe me, once one of these systems is installed you will have no lack of encouraged users to help you sell the idea to more skeptical colleagues.

Another promising area is intelligent forms. Instead of checking information after it is entered into an Engineering Change Order form, put an expert system into the form so it can check input as it is created, not hours or days later when the cost of finding an error is much greater.

THE RIGHT TOOL FOR THE JOB

The next thing to do is find the right tool. Since this is not a survey, I will only discuss those products that I have used. The important characteristics to look for in a product are idea structuring tools and integrated rules. Idea tools help structure knowledge into logical hierarchies, and rule sets help focus queries and add expert system capabilities to the final product.

One of the best tools for turning paper documentation into electrons is Guide, by InfoAccess Inc. (formerly Owl International). Ford Motor Company is using Guide to help service bay workers diagnose the ills of your car. Guide is a hypertext application that lets you import word-processed text or enter text directly into its editor. You can then transform your linear text into a non-linear tool. Information that is important to certain classes of users can be hidden behind buttons where it is easily accessible with a click of a mouse, but out of the way for those who don't need it. If you like glossaries but hate flipping to the end of a book to find a definition, Guide's Definition function will be a favorite. Any word in a document can be linked to a definition. One mouse click and the definition pop-ups up conveniently on the screen. When you release the mouse, the definition disappears.

Guide's most powerful function is Reference. By strategically employing this command you can skip from one point in a document to another with a single mouse click. Guide can be configured to keep track of most of your mouse activity so returning to any point in the text is easy. Guide also makes excellent use of graphics. On the Macintosh, using the Owl Desk Accessory known as Scribbler, you can create graphics that become interactive in Guide. Clicking elements in the graphic can display definitions or transport you to other reference points or documents. Guide is available on the Macintosh and on the PC under Windows. A recently released translation program allows you to convert between the two environments with a minimum cleanup. Both programs support runtime versions for delivery.

One of the most exciting opportunities in the hypertext arena is Apple's HyperCard. With HyperCard you can perform the same types of links found in Guide, but with a lot more freedom. Guide is hypertext; HyperCard is Hypermedia. By integrating HyperCard into your shop floor you could bring your documentation to life. Where a manual may have instructions about how to put something together, HyperCard and a CD-ROM could put video instructions on screen. Even a minimum configuration Macintosh can handle limited animation and voice-overs easily. Think about the opportunities for a manual that could talk someone through a repair operation and tell the technician when to look at the drawing.

HyperCard, as good as it is for documentation, is not really intelligent. You can intelligently create links, but that means you need to think of everything in advance. If only you could put an expert system inside HyperCard. With HyperX from Millennium Software and Nexpert Object from Neuron Data you can.

HyperX is written entirely in HyperTalk, HyperCard's programming language. The environment of if-then rules, agendas, and attribute-value pairs will be familiar territory to any AI hacker. HyperX is fully integrated into HyperCard, so it can be used to infer what document should be opened or what link to go to next. I have built a small preventative maintenance (PM) system using HyperX. The system walks you through the PM procedure, including what tapes and fixtures to load for tests and voice-overs if they are desired. When test results are reported to the system, it analyzes them for abnormality and then calls HyperX for analysis. HyperX recommends a repair and then calls another HyperCard document into which it records failure information and actions taken. The ability to link HyperX to the problem log stack took a little over an hour and completely eliminated the need for paper.

But HyperX may be underpowered for complex systems like F-14 jet fighters or complete manufacturing facilities. Into this niche comes Nexpert Object and its new HyperCard bridge. With the HyperCard Bridge, users of Nexpert can link complete knowledge bases into the HyperCard environment much as they would link Nexpert's AI libraries with a C program. Programming Nexpert to perform in HyperCard is not as easy as HyperX, but all of Nexpert's object-oriented approach and intricate inferencing options are supported. The HyperCard Bridge implementation is so flexible that new rules can be added to the system from within Hyper-Card. At RWD Technologies in Columbia, MD, Nexpert Object and HyperCard work with company databases to diagnose failures in line equipment based on defects in products. The RWD system supports on-line technical documentation and spare parts ordering information.

Tools for the PC

The Macintosh isn't your computer of choice for delivery of a shop floor application? On the PC you could use Knowledge Garden's KnowledgePro for developing applications much like those described above. KnowledgePro's programming language is no more difficult to learn than HyperTalk, and it equals it in power and flexibility.

Another suite of tools to consider on the PC are Neil Larson's MaxThink products. Structuring text files and PC Paint Brush files into his HyperRez memory resident application could bring much of the power of Hypertext to the shop floor with a minimum of expense. All of Neil's products take a bit of a brain tweaking before they sink in, but once you understand them, powerful systems will follow.

Structuring the Information

Well, so much for tools. Now we must structure the information. The basic unit for intelligent systems is the chunk. A knowledge chuck is a piece of information that wholly describes a thing or a function. If you are working on a motorcycle, the knowledge chunks would consist of the carburetor, the clutch, or the full pump. Interrelations between these chunks can then be defined and explicitly stated. Many of Neil Larson's MaxThink tools can help you define links and hone them down to their essence. For those of you who have dealt with relational databases, this type of analysis will be familiar. Your information will come from repair manuals and interviews with your experts. Much of intelligent documentation is knowledge engineering.

The final step is translating your chunks into the tool you have chosen. In Nexpert Object these chunks would be called objects; in HyperCard they could be called cards; in KnowledgePro they would be called topics.

Now Scanning, Sir

The biggest single chore after turning your chunks of information into logical structures is putting all of that information into the computer. Systems design deals primarily with classes of information, not the information itself. For a good system, much of what is in a manual still exists on the computer—it is just accessed differently. As recently as three years ago you would pay thousands and thousands of dollars to manually or electronically convert typewritten or printed information into computer format. Now the technologies are converging. As text retrieval systems become more adept at indexing and storing large amounts of text, relatively standard personal computers are being transformed into document conversion centers.

One of the most popular and most effective OCR systems is OmniPage by Caere Corporation. OmniPage is an optical character recognition package that works on both the Macintosh and PC compatibles. OmniPage requires increased memory and faster processors, but both are readily available and priced competitively. Documents placed into the scanner are digitized and then examined character by character for matches against an internal set of letter patterns. Tildes found on the screen after the examination represent letters that OmniPage could not identify. I have found OmniPage fast and fairly accurate. Most problems revolve around words that are slammed together or words where spaces have been inserted between letters. For most documents a few minutes of clean-up with your favorite word processor and spell checker will make acceptable text for your on-line system, although current versions of OmniPage now incorporate OCR-based spelling correctors and neural networks to increase accuracy. If you want an intelligent system and are willing to wait a little longer for your pages to process, you might want to look at AccuText from Xerox.

AccuText first examines a document for characters, then it kicks into AI mode and tries to identify words. The program searches its internal 50,000 word dictionary for words that match the patterns found in your document. Since AccuText recognizes not only characters, but words, it does not suffer from the two problems found in most OmniPage scanned documents. AccuText even learns fuzzy patterns that seem to represent a word consistently and uses those to help increase its identification speed.

There are several less expensive and less capable products on the market. These are the two that I have found work consistently and with little difficulty. Both systems work best with clean originals, but good copies often work just as well. I have over one-megabyte of AI material scanned into a personal database. I don't just use intelligent documentation systems in the oil-covered shop floor, I also put them to use on the messy, book-ridden desktops of my office at home.

Making Better Use of Knowledge

Hypertext and AI application on the shop floor are never inexpensive propositions. For them to be used effectively each user must be able to gain access to the information stored inside immediately. There should be a terminal at each work cell. The information should also be graphic where required and completely edited for accuracy everywhere. Neither graphic artists, draftspeople, or good copyeditors are easy to find. To have an effective system your company must be willing to invest in the project. When you are looked at like an idiot for proposing the end of the paper reign, back up your proposal with good return on investment calculations based on decreased line downs, improved product quality, and fuller utilization of people's talents. While a factory worker is repairing a broken conveyor, your manufacturing engineer can be learning new things to pass along to the documentation system.

Intelligent documentation systems are not meant to transform your work force into expert system-following dullards; they are meant to help elevate less-trained employees to their next level of performance.

PROCESS PLANNING 101

Rather than covering more products, let's turn our focus toward how to solve a particular problem in a particular industry. The problem is process planning and the industry is printed circuit board assembly manufacturing.

Their are many good books on how to generate process plans. Many articles and papers have been written focusing on process planning in metal fabrication or machine shops. I chose to look at printed circuit board assembly because it is the manufacturing area I am most familiar with and it is representative of most assembly operations—and besides, I get tired of reading about how to plan a gun barrel's honing.

What Is Process Planning?

Process planning for an assembly involves selecting the best combination of routes, work centers, tools, and processes for a particular board assembly. Good process planners ask several questions about the environment in which assembly takes place. What is the best machine for a particular task? Before which step and after which step must the current task be completed? Can the tasks ever be completed out of sequence? How much time will it take to complete the task?

Process planning is usually a job performed by manufacturing engineers. Manufacturing engineers design and implement factory equipment and play an important role in keeping a factory working once it is installed. They know better than anyone in the factory what the factory is capable of doing (although assembly workers often teach manufacturing engineers the realities of their new designs early in the life cycle of a process). In some companies, manufacturing engineers are either called, or joined by, process engineers. Process engineers, when they exist in their own right, are more closely related to particular process steps, rather than with the whole assembly line.

Process planning systems can be categorized as generative systems and variant systems. Generative systems examine the characteristics of an assembly and generate a new plan based on the systems knowledge of the manufacturing facility and its capabilities. A variant system stores several potential process plans and then matches an appropriate plan with the assembly. In this article we are going to concentrate on a modified variant model because it is easy to understand and will give us a good place to evolve from. The modified variant system takes a basic plan and modifies it to some extent based on the components in the assembly.

Basic Representation

There are three main representations in a process planning model: the factory line configuration; the parts, and the relationship of the parts to the assembly; and work center capabilities. The combination and interplay between these representations seek the optimal routing for a new assembly.

The line is a series of steps. In manufacturing systems, these steps are referred to as routers or routings. A routing is a specific and finite set of process steps an assembly must go through before it is complete. Routings typically contain automated steps and manual steps. The following list shows a typical configuration for a simple line.

Stockroom Kitting
Kit Preparation
Kit Audit
Board Loader
Screen Printer
Epoxy Dispenser
Pick and Place Machine 1
Pick and Place Machine 2
Oven
Post-IR Inspection
Manual Assembly
Wave Solder
Cleaner
Post-Wash Inspection
Final Assembly
In-Circuit Test
Burn-In
Functional Test
Inspection
Quality Assurance
Packaging

This simple representation of a production line as a series of steps associated with a line number forms the basic representation scheme of the system. It is from this assembly line and other prototypical assembly lines stored in the system, that the basic line configuration is chosen and the hours and costs are developed.

The primary goal of process planning is to link together the right mix of work centers, arrange them in sequence, and generate a file or report that can be input as the master routing file to a Material Requirements Planning (MRP) system or shop floor tracking system.

The first-class structure in the system is the machine or resource itself. Machines, or groups of like machines and resources, are usually called work centers. Work centers have operators, work cell assignments, maintenance schedules, and other elements associated with them. The following list shows a typical object schema for a work center.

Operator
Queue Time
Description
Manufacturer
Maintenance Schedule
Pay Class
Work Cell Assignment
Recommended Time
Minimum Time
Maximum Time
Productivity Allowance
Shift
Process Capability
Valid Succeeding Work Centers
Standard Cost
Standard Hours

The work center class maintains a slot with Valid Succeeding Work Centers. This slot ensures that only logical relationships are generated when the plan is modified. If a work center under consideration for insertion into the routing file is not a valid succeeding work center for the work center before it in the proposed plan, then it will not be inserted and a valid insertion point will be sought.

Parts are represented as a combination of CAD data and inventory data. Although all of the data is not necessarily used by the process planning system, future enhancements may take into account various parameters for choosing which parts are outside of manufacturing standards and which parts may present manufacturing difficulties. In the current design (see the following typical part master class schema list), only the class code, preparation code, and part number are used. (As an example of a future item, the vendor might be validated at planning time to make sure they still are approved in the Approved Vendor List (AVL). The X and Y coordinates might be used to validate if the prescribed parts are far enough apart so that no tooling conflicts occur during manufacturing.)

Part Number
Part Master Description
Inventory Parameters
ABC Code
Unit of Measure
Usage History
Source Code
Engineer
Process Type
Planner/Buyer
Material
Extended Description
Total Lead Time
Dock-to-Stock Lead Time
Inspection Lead Time
Average Cycle Time
Vendor
Class Code
X Coordinates
Y Coordinates
Chip Size (Area)
Preparation Code

The final item that requires representation is the assembly itself and the parts that make up the assembly. Assembly parts also include bills of material or BOMs. BOMs link several parts together to form an assembly. Assemblies usually consist of a hierarchical structure called the *indented part structure*. The highest level BOM may link several other BOMs together to form the final assembly. In automobile manufacturing, the car radio has a BOM and is made in a separate factory than the final automobile, but if you look at the car's indented part structure, the radio and all of its components will appear. It will look something like this:

Super Duper Car

1.1	Doors
1.2	Fenders
1.3	Hood
1.4	Tailgate

1.5   Mirror (drivers)
1.6   Mirror (passengers)
1.7   Mirror (rearview)
1.8   Radio
    2.1   Knob 1
    2.2   Knob 2
    2.3   PCB 1
    2.4   PCB 2
        3.1   IC 1
        3.2   IC 2
        3.3   Capacitor 1
        3.4   Resistor 1
        and so on …

This BOM illustrates some elements of a car and the assemblies of which it is composed. The lowest level assembly, PCB 2, is composed of 2 ICs, a capacitor, and a resistor. That is a typical, though very simple, board assembly we are going to learn to plan.

Almost all factories making board assemblies use single-level bills of material. This greatly simplifies the planning process. Rather than planning many operations, a single continuous process can be determined and applied.

The final line configuration plan will be represented by a sequential list of work centers, but unlike the work centers in a database file, the object representations will include precedence information. Not only will the work center know how long the work will be there and what it will cost, it will also know which station preceded it and what station succeeds it. A routing object definition looks like this:

Assembly Number
Work Center
Preceding Work Center
Succeeding Work Center
Processing Hours
Standard Cost for Assembly

The representation in this system will grow as it develops. This is a basic structure upon which the future will be built. Various classes may be created in the future to add deeper reasoning abilities to the system.

Processing Logic

Producing a plan using the combination of variant processing and automated modification is a rather simple process, but there are many hidden choices that need to be made. The complexity of the board components drives up the number of decisions that the system must make dramatically. The following steps outline a typical process flow.

1. The CAD database is combined with the Part Master Records from the MRP system. This links CAD data, such as X, Y coordinates and chip size with descriptions, part classes, and other information like vendor and planner codes.

2. The board elements are classified according to their part class and size. The parts are linked to new classes that identify their unique characteristics.

3. Based on the classifications, a board type is determined. The board type is based on the technology intended (through hole, surface-mount technology, or mixed) and chip categories.

4. A prototypical plan is selected, based on board classification, and read into memory from a database.

5. The parts in the assembly are linked to the appropriate work center for which they are intended. Some parts, like diodes or crystals, that require legs to be straightened or leads to be trimmed, may be linked to more than one operation. (These items are identified by the Preparation Code slot.)

6. Any parts not linked to the prototypical plan work centers are then matched against the set of work centers until a work center capable of placing the part is found. (An alternative to this step is to build a very large prototypical routing with all assemblies and include all work centers—step 7 remains

valid.) When a work center is identified, it is inserted into the appropriate place in the routing.

7. Other modifications may include manual swapping of chosen machines and the removal of unused work centers from the assembly routing.

8. The final routing is displayed, with those items changed highlighted. The engineer may click an item to display what was changed. The engineer may change any element of the plan at this point, if required.

9. Based on the validated and authorized plan, costs are determined for each operation. Parts are first linked to their standard cost element and then the cost is determined by multiplying the standard hours and the rate for the work center by the quantity and type of part being processed. This method processes work centers sequentially. Pay rates are retrieved from a payroll database.

10. Output hard copy and electronic versions of the new router.

That concludes the basic processing for our modified variant process planner. In the next section we will look at the details of this processing, including a close examination of actual rules and routines included in the system.

What's So AI About This?

Although most of this processing can be accomplished using a database, the "AI" part of this operation involves using heuristics to generalize the concepts. Rather than implicitly coding which machine can place a part into the part master records, this process-planning architecture maintains current machine capabilities. Its dynamic nature allows the system to match processes, new or old, with parts as they are created in the database. If new machines are added, single changes are required in the knowledge base, but part coding remains constant. If new part codes are invented, only the representations of the machine need to be changed, making maintenance very easy.

The choice of machine type is also a heuristic notion. If more than one machine is capable of placing a component, then heuristics in the system allow it to choose which machine is best for this particular part, or which machine is most compatible with the other machines and options already chosen or under investigation. By understanding which machines may be legally linked to each other, the system avoids making sequencing errors.

Management Considerations

Data. Clean data is essential to the effective use of any automated system like this one. The past classifications and the descriptions of the objects all have a major impact on the quality of the plan. If the class codes are inaccurate, you may not only generate invalid plans, but valid plans may reflect false costs because parts are accumulated and charged to the wrong work center.

I have worked on 15 MRP systems. I have rarely seen one with data that matched the cleanliness of a Marriott non-smoking room. Somewhere in the database, and usually more places than one can count in a week, the specter of carelessness disrupts the continuity. Wisps of inaccuracy float up and down the system affecting inventory, work in process, and material plans.

Before you automate any processes, be prepared for the data problems that are in your current database. You may spend more time in meetings discussing data integrity than the integrity of you and your expert system.

The Future of Process Planning

Knowledge-based process planning systems still have a way to go. We have only looked at one small design, but it shows the weaknesses of even the most robust systems. There is very little this system can do to modify the process and know that it has created a good plan. This system, as described, will generate a valid plan, but it may not be a good plan.

The system also lacks the ability to learn from the past. There is currently no mechanism in the system for writing a new library object set if the new plan is a significant variant on an old model.

Future systems should be able to recognize that a new plan is a major change and record it for posterity, and reuse.

Although object-oriented representations are employed in this system, the primary logic engine consists of rules. Future systems should take the next object-oriented step and imbue the objects themselves with the ability to negotiate with their neighbors for a place in the sequential outline of the factory.

The idea of using class codes for classification of parts and boards is very similar to another AI/CAM idea called group technology. Group technology employs more elaborate coding schemes than the one presented here, but it is essentially a way of grouping parts into logical families for use in the deduction of several manufacturing attributes, including process plans. But as I wrote this section of the chapter, it struck me that neural networks might be a logical, and better, answer to the classification system. A backward propagation neural network, trained on various board types, could easily identify a type of board and save many minutes or hours of complex pattern matching.

PROCESS PLANNING 102

Having just discussed the general attributes of a process planning system, and having begun thinking out loud about how one should be implemented, I'll continue with that theme here and provide some real world experiences and discussions of what happened when I actually tried to implement my ideas.

Reality Is Stranger Than Fiction

When you start thinking about an expert system, everything is clear. As you start developing one, however, initial thoughts often fade into obscurity. The details of slot methods and the interaction between them are difficult to imagine—and the ideas so structured and sensible on paper simply do not work when actually applied (see the section, "Programming Technique").

The classes presented in "Process Planning 101" required augmentation as I continued to develop the system. Items like Class_Code_Cost were added to store additional information about the process. During implementation it became clear that atomic read to individual records was stressing my disk drive, so I decided to load the entire set of cost records into memory just prior to using them.

The other significant change involves the use of Master_Routing and Planned_Routing classes. Master_Routing is the class to which sequences are initially assigned. During processing destructive evaluation either removes a sequence from Master_Routing, or attaches it to the Planned_Routing class for costing and final report preparation.

The heuristics for a production system would be much more complicated than those employed in this prototype. Thousands of parts exist and hundreds of categories for those parts. Manufacturing lines are also more dynamic than those found in this prototype.

Despite those shortcomings, this system represents the complex reasoning and programming required in a full production quality process planning system. The techniques have been discovered; now what remains is the customization of the system to fit individual manufacturing lines, types of parts, and varieties of bills of material.

Processing Facts

The processing flow chart in the previous section turned out to be pretty close to the final product. Here is a recap of that process with a few more of the actual implementation details.

Start System and Load Data

The system is started by suggesting a single backward chaining rule. In the prototype this rule requests the assembly to be planned and validates it against a part number database. If the assembly is not found (meaning that the assembly is not a valid part number or does not qualify as an assembly), the system asks for another assembly part number.

Once the identity of the assembly is established, the system goes to the bill of material file and loads the appropriate bill of material for the assembly. The current implementation only works with single-level bills of material. An assumption is made that the bill of material file used is a special file consisting of CAD and material data that has been collected, collated, and validated prior to use by the process planner.

When the parts are loaded, they are linked to the PART and BOM_PART classes as well as to the current assembly object. This flexible class hierarchy provides multiple paths to certain questions that could be implemented in the system. (Part information helps determine the machine that will place the part. Aggregate part information collects in the assembly object through its link to the bill of material.)

Classify Board

Once all the parts are in the system, processing continues by classification of the bill of material structure, based on component types. The number of components in a class are counted and loaded into system variables. Table 4.1 lists those parts that the current prototype acknowledges.

Table 4.1: Class Codes

Class Code	Description	Type
Class_Code_1	Standard chip	SMT
Class_code_2	Through hole IC	TH
Class_code_3	PLCC44	SMT
Class_Code_4	PLCC68	SMT
Class_Code_5	PLCC100	SMT
Class_Code_6	Crystal	Manual
Class_Code_7	Diode	Manual
Class_Code_8	Speaker	Manual
Class_Code_9	Dip switch	SMT
Class_Code_10	Connector	Manual
Class_Code_99	Assembly	Assembly

Here is the listing of the classification rule:

```
RULE : Rule 1
If
  step.next is "classify parts"
Then Classification_started.hypo
  is confirmed.
  And LENGTH(<IClass_code_1I>) is assigned to class_code_eval.class_code_1
  And LENGTH(<IClass_code_2I>) is assigned to class_code_eval.class_code_2
  And LENGTH(<IClass_code_3I>) is assigned to class_code_eval.class_code_3
  And LENGTH(<IClass_code_4I>) is assigned to class_code_eval.class_code_4
  And LENGTH(<IClass_code_5I>) is assigned to class_code_eval.class_code_5
  And LENGTH(<IClass_code_6I>) is assigned to class_code_eval.class_code_6
  And LENGTH(<IClass_code_7I>) is assigned to class_code_eval.class_code_7
  And LENGTH(<IClass_code_8I>) is assigned to class_code_eval.class_code_8
  And LENGTH(<IClass_code_9I>) is assigned to class_code_eval.class_code_9
  And LENGTH(<IClass_code_10I>) is assigned to class_code_eval.class_code_10
  And
  class_code_eval.class_code_1+class_code_eval.class_code_3+class_code_eval.class
  _code_4+class_code_eval.class_code_5+class_code_eval.class_code_9 is assigned
  to class_code_eval.smt_qual
  And class_code_eval.class_code_2 is assigned to class_code_eval.TH_qual
  And
  class_code_eval.class_code_6+class_code_eval.class_code_7+class_code_eval.class
  _code_8+class_code_eval.class_code_10 is assigned to class_code_eval.man_qual
  And step.next is set to "Load plan"
```

This rule counts the number of parts in each class code. The summary of related class codes determines the types of technology employed on the board (that is, through hole, surface-mount technology, and manual). The final line changes the value of step.next to "Load Plan," and forces forward chaining to the rule for loading the plan, which has IS STEP.NEXT "LOAD PLAN" as its first condition.

Select Plan

Based on the results of the classification, one of the four plans (through hole, SMT and through hole, pure SMT or mixed SMT, or through hole and manual) is retrieved from the plan SYLKDB database and loaded into the system. The sequence information in the plan is attached to the Master_Routing class.

Validate Plan

The objects attached to the Master_Routing class are evaluated from smallest to largest, based on their sequence numbers. Currently the system supports a single external validation function. If purchased parts are delivered directly to the line rather than being pulled from stores, then all operations associated with the stockroom and kitting operation are removed from the Master_Plan class and eliminated from the system completely.

Component information determines the validity of each sequence. If the current work center under evaluation is not valid, it is either destroyed or changed to a more appropriate work center. If SMT components are present, then the SMT Pick and Place Machines found in the prototypical plan are validated. If the number of components for a pick and place sequence exceed the capability of the machine, a warning message is generated telling the planner that the sequence is not viable. Upon validation, the sequence objects are deleted from the Master_Routing class and attached to the Planned_Routing class.

For pick and place equipment, the number of components required for the assembly are compared to the capability of the given machine. If there is a discrepancy between the number of components and a machine's capability, a warning object is created and attached to the class Warnings, along with the descriptor of the warning (for example, "Too many parts").

Cost Plan

When the length of the Master_Routing class reaches 0, the system continues into the costing module. Plan costing begins by loading all work centers from the work center file. As in the plan validation sequence, each item in the Planned_Routing file is evaluated. Rather than using the destructive list manipulation present in the validation module, plan costing evaluates to lowest-level sequence number without a cost, until all sequences have a cost. Here is a typical costing example for the function test work center:

```
If
   step.next is "cost next"
   And \cost_account_vars.current_seq\.work_center is "Functional test"
   And <|Part|>.class_code is not "class_code_99"
Then costing.hypo
   is confirmed.
   And ((LENGTH(<|Part|>)*0.05)/60) is assigned to
\cost_account_vars.current_seq\.processing_hours
   And Reset cost_account_vars.reset_var
   And cost_account_vars.reset_var is assigned to cost_account_vars.reset_var
```

The equation looks at the length of the complete parts list. It is currently assumed that all parts on the assembly must pass functional test and that it takes .05 seconds per board component to test the board. The result is divided by 60 to yield the standard number of hours for assembly.

The if-change method of the sequence's processing hours slot is invoked after the standard processing hours are determined. This forces the multiplication of the processing hours and the pay class for the object. The pay class is derived from the work center object associated with the current sequence's work center number.

Write the Report

When all items in the Planned_Routing class have a cost, the final plan is written to disk. This plan includes the name of the object in the Planned_Routing class, the sequence number, the work center, the processing hours, the standard costs for assembly, and the assembly number. This file is stored in SYLKDB format.

Programming Technique

An expert system shell is an excellent place to apply knowledge to a problem, but it is often a difficult place to apply procedural techniques. The examples here, provided in Nexpert Object format, reflect a few of the programming tricks used to implement this system.

Processing the work centers required recursive programming. Nexpert has no facilities for explicitly writing for...while loops, so a knowledge-based technique must be employed. Basically, this involves checking the length of the list of objects remaining in the class Master_Routing. While that list remains greater than 0, Nexpert continues to process work centers. That sounds simple enough until you ask what the next work center is.

```
If
    step.next is "validate plan"
    And LENGTH(<|Master_Routing|>) is greater than 0
Then validation1.hypo
    is confirmed.
    And System_Vars.current_seq is assigned to System_Vars.current_seq
```

This is the rule that checks the length of the list. The assignment of System_vars.current_seq to itself forces the order-or-sources slot to find a value. Initially the list is whole and the order-or-sources method evaluates to the smallest numbered item in the Master_Routing class and then converts its integer value to a string. When System_Vars.current_seq is completed, finding a value, that value is always different. The change of value invokes the if-change method of the slot and appends the string "SEQ_" to itself. It then changes the value of step.next, which places rules with step.next in their conditions on the agenda.

```
System_Vars.current_seq
ORDER OF SOURCES :
Do  INT2STR(MIN(<|Master_Routing|>.Sequence))
  SELF.current_seq
IF CHANGE DO :
    Do  STRCAT("SEQ_",SELF.current_seq)
  SELF.current_seq
    Let  step.next     "Choose Validation"
```

On the next pass and all passes after the first one, the system must reset itself and get ready for a changed world. This rule typifies the situation:

```
If
   step.next is "Choose Validation"
   And kitting_vars.purchased is "No"
   And \System_Vars.current_seq\.work_center is "Kit Preparation"
Then validation2.hypo
   is confirmed.
   And System_Vars.create_plan is assigned to System_Vars.create_plan
   And System_Vars.reset_var is assigned to System_Vars.reset_var
```

If kitting is "NO," meaning that the material is handled normally by the stockroom, then the work center Kit Preparation is determined to be valid. Validation of a work center sets several housekeeping functions into motion. The first functions invoked are found in System_Vars.create_plan.

```
System_Vars.create_plan
ORDER OF SOURCES :
    RunTimeValue "OK"
IF CHANGE DO :
    Let \System_Vars.current_seq\.processed  "Yes"
    CreateObject \System_Vars.current_seq\   |Planned_Routing|
    DeleteObject \System_Vars.current_seq\   |Master_Routing|
    Reset   System_Vars.reset_var
```

This method defaults to "OK" and does nothing in the system except encapsulate the functions required to link and unlink a work center from classes. Resetting System_Vars.reset_var prepares the slot for the next work center. This is a very efficient use of code because it requires definition only once. It can be thought of as a Nexpert subroutine. Once the housekeeping for classes is complete, the whole system must be reset to get ready for the next work center.

```
System_Vars.reset_var
ORDER OF SOURCES :
    Let    SELF.reset_var "Validate plan"
IF CHANGE DO :
    Do     SELF.reset_var SELF.reset_var
    Let    step.next "Validate plan"
    Reset  validation1.hypo
    Reset  SELF.current_seq
    Reset  SELF.create_plan
```

Like the previous method, this one encapsulates several items that would otherwise appear in the action portion of each rule that required them. The methods are generic. Object-oriented-like message passing (via Nexpert's DO operator) invokes the methods. The System_vars.reset_var method resets the remaining system variables and rules so that they can be properly re-fired and re-instantiated for the next work center.

If the resets did not occur, Nexpert would assume that the truth of validation2.hypo established in the kit preparation hypothesis is all that was required and end processing. By resetting the variables and forcing their reevaluation, Nexpert reexamines its world based on the changes made in the structure of the class lists.

The heuristics of the system are very flat. Very little backward chaining is used in the knowledge representation. All rules for either work center validation or costing are all attached to the same hypothesis for loop processing. This technique provides an easy way to visually see the heuristics and their relationships. The flatness of the rule bases makes adapting to new situations less investigative.

Facing the User

I developed the initial prototype of the system exclusively in the Nexpert development environment. But after reflecting on how bored I got running test, I decided to develop a more elaborate interface for the system. Nexpert runs under Apple's HyperCard as an X Command. All of Nexpert's development capabilities are directly accessible from HyperCard or can be simulated using a combination of Nexpert calls and Hypertalk scripts.

The navigation window allows direct access to various process planning functions across cards. Using the navigation palette saved programming time and disk space by removing all card-specific links and their buttons. The first stack of the card starts Nexpert, creates the Nexpert handlers, loads the knowledge base, and initiates processing. When questions are required, the stack contains cards with names equal to the Nexpert slot requiring a value. Buttons on the card send data to the Nexpert inference kernel.

When processing is completed, HyperCard begins an interactive inquiry session with Nexpert that builds a graphic representation of the line. From sequence number buttons, Nexpert objects may be queried about the value of their slots. The system also contains a cost analysis card that asks Nexpert to provide the costs associated with each routing sequence. When the cost information is returned, and the relative percentages of each sequence's costs are computed, the end user may create a pie chart for easier visualization of the cost elements.

HyperCard proved to be a rapid and accurate prototyping environment. It took less than 30 hours to create the complete Hyper-Card environment, including help and debugging facilities.

It All Stacks Up

There are several things that I don't like about the implementation of this system. The costing information is all rule driven. Perhaps future implementations will later include a generic costing object method that uses the same set of methods to cost all types of parts. It appears that a richer data set is needed to create this type of costing capability.

Overall, however, I found Nexpert and HyperCard a powerful team for implementing this system. I used years of notes for expertise and gathered various papers on the subject to validate my tact. The implementation of the system was much more difficult than I first imagined, but a 120-hour expert prototype is still a small system. Some of the systems I have worked on took well over a year before we had a proof of concept.

THE OBJECT OF DESIGN

"The objects are coming, the objects are coming!" yelled Paul Cobol on his famous midnight ride. The battle raged for years—first spaghetti code, then structured programming—and one by one the older languages entered the fray. "Defeat the objects," Paul exclaimed.

Paul Cobol's message was more prophesy than a call to arms. Despite the years of debate and denial, objects are infiltrating manufacturing and business systems. Objects, like many new technologies, enter factories not through the door of MIS, but through portals of engineering.

The Object of CAD

CAD and OOP were destined to collide. CAD systems deal with design objects. What better way to implement design objects than with software objects? CAD tools represent parts, relationships between parts, the attributes of parts, pictures of parts, and general business information. Current CAD stations only allow designers to draw, and sometimes, query a drawing's geometry. Imagine an interactive, intelligent CAD station. Imagine working with a system that contains information about your product, previous products, and a multitude of characteristics about component parts and materials.

An OOP language, with user-defined relationships, proves an overwhelming choice for CAD development. CAD requires access to past designs and access to current manufacturing technology for validation. CAD systems work with representations of real-world objects that contain many descriptors and behaviors. CAD systems need inheritance, libraries, polymorphism, and encapsulation—the fundamentals of OOP.

Storing Your World

The world revolves around us with marvelous simplicity, as long as we don't look too closely. Hidden in every integrated circuit, sheet metal case, or transformer is data and process. A simple Winchester disk drive controller board contains more than just its function and its serial number. Someone spent hundreds of hours transforming the idea of a Winchester disk drive controller board into a coherent design.

Designers require data about shapes, sizes, capabilities, and hazards before they start the design process. Interactive CAD will include information from many of these broad classes:

Material performance
Materials
Previous designs
Vendor facts and performance
Design rules
Manufacturing processes

General knowledge about the physical world
Functional requires
Manufacturing constraints
Test constraints
Part libraries
Cost constraints
Customer specifications
Business goals and objectives

Databases only serve as a starting point. Interactive CAD systems will require software that turns this data into decisions.

Interactive Thinking

The adventure of new product design forces reflection and analysis. As products become more complex, we perform more and more analysis. With the new emphasis on quality, qualification of a design becomes imperative. Problems discovered in manufacturing simply cost too much. In the darkness of our CAD rooms, we commune with computers. Today's CAD systems, however, return very little for our mental investment.

Solidifying a design often means bringing together a team of senior engineers—an often costly proposition. Customers demand high-quality, reliable products at reasonable prices. Concurrent engineering programs involve manufacturing, accounting, and marketing. Concurrency is not inexpensive, as many departments send representatives to meetings, or make them available to designers as required. Concurrent engineering, however, does yield improved products. For firms with high turnover, many products, or low employee commitment, concurrent engineering efforts often disband as momentum wanes.

Improved communication still produces organizational boundaries. Manufacturing still finds design flaws the first time two drilled aluminum plates meet on the factory floor. Engineering change orders, overtime labor, and incorrect inventory increase costs. Only melding manufacturing knowledge with design will reduce time-to-product and time-to-revenue periods.

Future electronic design stations, with intelligent object representations, will include cooperative processes that help the designer

make choices. The following list outlines the significant features for
an electronic assembly design station:

Cost Analysis
Part Selection
Thermal Analysis
Stress Analysis
Inventory Reduction Analysis
Manufacturing Analysis
Design for Assembly Advice
Parts and Relationships
Vendor Suggestions
Sub-Product Design Synthesis
Like Design Matching

The process of interactive design only creates a product with
attributes. For the conceptual design to become a complete product,
several processes must transform its data, and its very idea. The mass
of lines must become solder traces, and the CAD symbols must
become parts soldered to the board.

CAD By-Products

Significant CAD by-products include process plans, work instructions, cost estimates, bills of material, and other manufacturing documents. These documents and programs exist because humans analyze
CAD data and bestow it with manufacturing information.

With OOP technology, these by-products of CAD systems come
from encapsulated procedures attached to the objects. Printed circuit board assemblies, for instance, would include procedures on
how to write a process plan. Individual parts might include procedures and data to support process planning. Integrated circuits
encode height, width, and depth with special solder requirements or
offset bounds that identify components too close together.

With a rich data model, all information required to create manufacturing documentation should exist within the knowledge representation. From business policies to inventory goals, the information
about the world intrudes on the design so it won't ruin the product
during production.

The Object of the Lesson

Consider a typical engineer facing a typical engineering problem: *How do I select the right parts to make this new meter?* We will focus on the printed circuit board inside that meter to illustrate how objects work to aid the design engineer.

The CAD station screen ignites with horizontal strokes of citron and indigo, sapphire and vermilion. The integrated CAD program launches while an object database and a few dozen classes ready themselves for work. The engineer selects his global constraints like the name of the customer (which invokes customer-imposed constraints) and the design influence (design for cost, design for reliability, design for manufacturing, and so on). The engineer then enters the functional requirements into the system. All previous designs exist as objects in the design knowledge base. The system selects the most likely designs that provide the same functions your customer requires.

From the list of previous designs, the engineer selects one to change or creates a new one. We will assume the engineer wants to alter an older design. This meter must work faster, which requires a more powerful CPU. The system substitutes the 12 MHz 80286 chip with a 33 MHz 80386. The system then selects qualified components to enhance board functions. A faster clock may result in changes to other devices, like dynamic RAM—for example, 80ns DRAM replaces 120ns DRAM.

The objects themselves cooperate. The designer plays referee and judge. Subtle functional nuances introduce complexities that the system refers to its human partner. Information architecture and the human mind work as a team.

Once the design is complete, the system checks it against the functional requirements. Behavioral information in each part class facilitates the simulation. The function of the board becomes the logic of the board. The logic of the board becomes the detailed design. The logic diagram of an IC is another view of the IC. In the designer's view, he or she works with a pad pattern. In the simulators view, that pad pattern is a tree of AND/OR gates and other binary options.

When the board performs to specification, the system requests a manufacturing validation. This involves creation of a bill of material, test program, process plan, and cost estimate. The bill of material, including spatial relationships and parent/child relationships, drives the manufacturing planner.

The planner method determines what production line should make the board. The line profile loads into memory. The methods then determine if any part locations or proximities violate constraints. The test method generates a test or reviews the test programs for adequate test coverage of the board's logic. Cost methods examine material and process and seek those that defy prescribed profitability profiles.

As with all processes, iterations follow. The object-oriented intelligence at work in this design increases the process dramatically. Because the information about the business reacts with the information about the part, concurrency is common practice.

Today we spend hours trying to make manufacturing people speak loudly enough so that engineers will hear them. Manufacturing people will maintain the manufacturing knowledge in our future CAD environment. An object-oriented design tool makes manufacturing knowledge an integral part of the design tool, not a post-design afterthought. The completed design schedules itself into the factory, and several other objects act upon it there.

Executing the Objects

Objects represent both the physical and the conceptual. A part is a part object, but the idea of a transaction is also an object. Objects communicate with each other through message passing. An assembly object, whose assembly requires a replacement part, sends a replacement request to stockroom via a MaterialRequest object—the real world mimicked in an electronic counterpart.

Unlike the real world, no paper changes hands. No request stacks gather dust for days while inventory carrying costs multiply and incomplete assemblies litter the production line. Objects introduce the simultaneous execution of need.

The modeling of business rules extends from traditional relations to complex interactions. Not only is the need for a transaction captured in object relationship, but the procedures required to execute tasks also reside in the representation. The assembly not only knows it needs a transaction record, the transaction record understands how to communicate the transaction to the AGV in the stockroom.

Enterprise Representation

Perhaps the largest benefit of OOP technology comes from consistent, deep representations of the entire enterprise. It is very difficult for any COBOL or FORTRAN program to encompass the meaning, behavior, and data of an enterprise. OOP, be it C++, CLOS, Flavors, or an OODBMS, possesses the ability to capture the basic structure of the business in a single representation.

In most current databases, portions of the business reside outside the context of the corporate database. Material planning data, product structures, purchasing data, and cost data usually make it into a single database. Flat files or relational databases, however, are incapable of capturing the subtleties of the business. Relational databases loose the connections and interactions found in real-world objects. Businesses are extremely complex entities that require extremely complex representations.

Most AI programs see the world as a tightly focused beam of information, without temporal meaning or cause-effect context. But the AI community knows the world is more complex than tables. Most expert-system shells contain some level of frame support and many include rich object environments or extended frames. Research, like Enterprise Integration Technologies' LISP-based business prototype or Ontek's PACIS business representation, point to a new future. The explicit interplay of motion, thought, and physical reality reveal new understandings about the business, its processes, and its data. The analysis required to implement these systems forces manufacturing companies to examine their foundations. Achieving the promises of the computer industry requires new applications of computing technology. Objects and AI will meet to create autonomous computers systems.

The Object of It All

The next generation of software depends on objects. The business systems we dream of require autonomy of purpose. Real-time business systems must make their own decisions. Overhead costs in manufacturing drive the price of products to non-competitive heights. The handling of paper becomes absurd. Objects will help liberate manufacturing from nonvalue-added work. The real work of manufacturing is making and innovating products—software will never fully replace this task. Intelligent objects will save us from costly mistakes like reinventing an existing component or product. The tasks supporting manufacturing require extensive reengineering. As companies launch business practice reform efforts, objects, with their capability to capture and mimic the world, will become the heirs of the business system.

OPENING UP TO CLOS

In this era of open, standards-based client/server computing, standard languages only marginally support the goals of interoperability and interchangeability. Although COBOL, FORTRAN, and C all boast acceptance by standard bodies, their aging procedural paradigms do little to support rapid prototyping, intelligent applications, and software reuse. Only one object-oriented language has achieved standardom, the Common LISP Object System (CLOS), perhaps the most mature of the OO languages.

Very rarely does CLOS rear its head in corporate competitions. PowerBuilder, Visual Basic, Smalltalk, C++, even COBOL wage development tool wars on the battlefield of corporate MIS departments. CLOS is nowhere to be seen. Why?

Perhaps the first reason is AI. LISP is remembered by many MIS managers as the laboriously slow, machine-specific language that thrust AI into the abyss. Great names like Symbolics and LISP Machines promised a future of intelligent software. They delivered a few promising starts, but mostly found ways to turn the hair of shareholders a lighter shade of gray.

Another reason for CLOS's lack of appeal comes from LISP itself. LISP is the clay of the programming world. It is self-referential, interpreted, and very strange to look at, at least for a procedural programmer. So like Smalltalk, CLOS finds resistance among those tied to the traditions of the mainframe and minicomputer. Main event loops, GOSUBs, and GOTOs—these are structured programming and waterfall methodologies.

At this point in the history of programming, I find little comfort in structured programming. High-level tools like PowerBuilder and Visual Basic turn programmers loose to experiment, evolve, retract, and transform. A dozen iterations of a single screen in a single day.

Accelerating demands for quality software written in a short period of time has driven corporations toward lower expectations for their software. GUIs and databases alone do not make an infrastructure for the next millennium. Software that supports knowledge work requires intelligence and integration. Procedures will turn to heuristics, data to information and knowledge. Software needs to learn and to guess. And with the physical and logical distribution of corporations, software needs to collaborate over time and space as much as the humans that employ it.

The high cost of manufacturing equipment once constrained innovation in companies by locking them to archaic methods for too long. It may well be that software will be the lock-in technology that stunts the growth of corporations, eventually leading to their demise. How willing will companies be to change an enterprise system after investing several million dollars? It will take more than objects to enable adaptation in software.

Getting LISP out of the CLOSet

In 1995 The X3 Secretariat announced that LISP/CLOS joined the ranks of ANSI standard languages. The X3J13 technical finally completed its task. Neither C++ or Smalltalk have found the will in their programming elite to pound out a standard. Granted, in took years for LISP. Perhaps now is the time to reconsider using a standards-based language in your standards-based architecture.

But why CLOS? First, CLOS is a dynamic, fluid, and extremely robust language. The latest versions of LISP need only modest hardware to run. Character-based muLISP90 from Soft Warehouse (in Honolulu, Hawaii) runs on a low-end 386 and fits on a single 1.4MB floppy. Although muLISP90 doesn't ship with graphical editors, GUI builders, visual debuggers, and other accoutrements of its larger cousins, it exhibits the basic attributes of modern LISP in compact form.

Larger implementations of LISP do require a good deal of memory, a fast processor, and a speedy, spacious hard disk. A modern LISP implementation doesn't stretch a computer's capabilities any more than of other memory and disk-intensive environments like Microsoft Office. Smalltalk patrons and those running multiple clients with several layers of middleware have also found more of everything is better. Modern hardware is well prepared for modern LISP.

CLOS CLOSe-Up

Like all good object-oriented languages, CLOS supports the expected structures. Classes lead to instances populated with values in slots. Methods describe the behavior of objects. But LISP brings several things to the programming party that other languages have yet to discover.

Unlike other OO languages, CLOS allows for the creation and modification of classes and methods on the fly—not just instances, classes, and methods. If you are developing an application that needs to adapt over time, creating new classes during runtime is ideal. There is no need to limit the domain to the initial analysis. The domain of information represented can grow during runtime.

Early versions of objects in LISP, like Flavors, went down the traditional OO mechanics by using messages to invoke methods. CLOS chose to abandon messages in favor of tighter integration with LISP. CLOS borrows functions from LISP. Method definition results in a generic function. Once a method is defined, it is evaluated by name. The generic function determines the behavior based on the provided arguments and classes involved in invocation. Generic function-based methods look very much like standard LISP code. No new data manipulation methods are defined.

A Flavors instantiation and method call might look like this:

```
(setq orange-hat (make-instance 'hat :color 'orange :brim
    'wide))
(send orange-hat :tip)
```

Flavors requires a somewhat stilted syntax (stilted at least in LISP).

In CLOS the same scene might look like this:

```
(setq orange-hat (make-instance 'hat :color 'orange :brim
    'wide))
(tip orange-hat)
```

The CLOS solution appears like any other LISP function, with generic functions working its magic behind the parentheses, determining which *tip* I mean based on the object class and data provided. As the result of this tight integration with LISP, generic functions can be used as the first argument in **apply** and **funcall** like any other like function.

Although Smalltalk is a dynamic environment, it does not benefit from the software clay metaphor so often ascribed to LISP. The very structure of classes generic to Smalltalk remove much of the language's spontaneity. LISP is a massive, complex, loose, and often confusing compendium of ideas from forty years of computing. But LISP is also often elegant, sparse, and poetic when crafted by an artist. CLOS embraces all of LISP's strengths, including symbolic manipulation and the ability to model heady concepts—and it adds object features that help make LISP's often abstract data definitions more concrete.

Just being a powerful language is not enough, people have to use it—and CLOS is indeed finding fans in both government and business.

All Is Not CLOSt

Although much of corporate America shies away from LISP and its AI roots, the federal government, AI's greatest benefactor, continues to reap what it has sown. The Hubble Space Telescope relies on the CLOS-based SPIKE system to schedule time on its much sought after instrument array. SPIKE performs dynamic scheduling that takes into account actual observation completion, viewing conditions, object positioning, and other factors. Other aerospace applications include the Boeing 777 and F-22, which owe much of their design to CLOS-base engineering tools.

In the commercial world, Price Waterhouse uses its CLOS-based Planet application to assist auditors in planning audits while the model-based reasoning system, Comet, evaluates a client's financial control processes from flowcharts and other documents already generated by auditors.

In the tool arena, Blackboard Technologies Group uses CLOS for the implementation of its software collaboration tool, GBB. With GBB objects communicate on a virtual blackboard, posting their information and retrieving data from other objects as they need it.

A smattering of applications and a taste of capability is probably not enough to persuade you to desert the onslaught of C++, Power-Builder, and Visual Basic that has gripped your development team. As we find need for applications that are more than widgets, algorithms, and database manipulation tools, the legacy of LISP will reassert itself into strategic systems. Even if AI never delivers on its promises, we will still need sophisticated systems that can adapt to environmental changes even before we do. Applications that learn and change need a language like LISP—and CLOS will be there to add the value of reuse and concrete representations to these next-generation symbolic applications.

REDEFINING KNOWLEDGE

Corporate America, like much of America, is looking for its soul, its heart, and its mind, all at the same time. Rapid technology advances, increasingly compact population centers, and new biological discoveries shake society to the edge of convergence or dissolution. The local newscasts televise drive-by shootings, voter apathy, and drug use to confirm suspicions about the horrors of change. Large corporations, despite layoffs and trade deficits, seem immune and resilient. Profits increase, stock values rocket to new records. But in the hallways, discussions about goals, objectives, and deadlines reveal strain. Long work hours, interpersonal isolation, and the demand that even the lowest-ranking members of the corporate hierarchy continually learn reengineered processes and supporting technologies has kindled a search for new ways to resonate with peers, customers, and partners.

Japan resonates with process. Process success represents higher honor than financial or performance success. To do the thing right is more important than doing the right thing. In America, we measure success as increased value or wealth. Process be damned. We are a nation of tinkerers and inventors. If the process does not work, we invent a unique solution that acts for that moment alone, destined to disappear from personal and collective memory. We abhor documentation, but we are prolific gadflies, in both verbal gossip and e-mail repartee. We write many things once, venture opinions at a moments notice, but retain little that can be considered long term wisdom. At the end of thirty, forty-five, or ninety days our e-mail returns to unorganized bits, and along with it, our opinions on designs and data, people, and process. America values results over process.

Knowledge fuels results. Everything from innovative product designs to brilliant competitive moves rely on knowledge. Knowledge has always been an underlying component of business, but one that simply existed, unlike production and capital, which require management and nurturing. Knowledge now asserts itself as nearly tangible. High-end talent shifts from company to company. Organizations scramble to record and preserve history from factory floor to boardroom. With knowledge management America seeks synergy between process and ambition, and hopes to find its heart and soul along the way.

Reinterpreting Knowledge

To most readers of this book, rules and objects store fragments of knowledge pontificated by experts during knowledge acquisition sessions. Knowledge management means applying version control and configuration management to rules and objects. Knowledge from interviews distills into explicit logic. Logic manifests in webs of connections, fact leading to fact—assertions exert themselves and lead to a conclusion, or drop off the edge of the domain, confusion masked in ignorance. But even when edges feather into obscurity, the logic remains pristine. Mathematics even define uncertainty.

The knowledge management of the '90s strays far from order or logic. Modern knowledge management combines traditional learning with chaos and complexity theory to form a self-organizing mélange where seemingly unrelated domains find fresh kinship.

Knowledge management attempts to store, distribute, and generate innovative ideas. Order and logic give way to intuition. Knowledge management centers as much on interpersonal sharing and personal release as it does on tools or databases. People and applications find order as needed, and the sharing of that order increases knowledge. Knowledge management remains adaptable, encompassing broadly divergent concepts. It eschews classification, redefining itself as constantly as the roots of its moniker.

Where knowledge engineering nurtures fact and experience into Aristotelian precision, knowledge management tends to view technology as a way of finding order in chaos. Knowledge management seeks to digitize and capture raw knowledge: digital recordings of dialog, scraps of scanned newspaper, discussion database banter, edicts and opinions conferred in e-mail, and video conversations captured as QuickTime movies.

Objects store raw data and metadata. Rules seek patterns among ever-changing repositories. Knowledge sources seldom reconcile or converge. Disagreement and disparity abound. Knowledge constantly accumulates. Relevant tidbits form relationships to general concepts. Related snippets present themselves just in time to assist with the question at hand. Patterns reveal themselves and the raw data becomes assimilated epiphany. Hundreds of divergent sources reveal, in their unique proximity, a potential for revelation. Data and information find context.

AI and expert systems tried to force all of knowledge into the singular construct of logic. The human mind is an excellent tool of logic, but logic is not its only province, nor perhaps even its most potent example. Logic fails to connect disparate sources, emotions, biases, and intuitions. It is not enough, in an expert systems development project, to know that an expert has some opinion about something, but that a line of reasoning supports the opinion. In other words, that some logic exists. So in fact, the opinion is not just opinion, but as close to fact as can possibly be derived. In *Star Trek IV*, Doctor McCoy turns to a frustrated Spock, who is about to calculate a time travel jump in which many of the variables have changed and the amount of change is unknown. McCoy tells Spock that his guesses are as good as many people's facts.

Everything is context. Spock's guesses, though fictional, derive from experience. And although the root experience may be lost, if someone is trusted, their opinion, however they derived it, is enough. Expert-system credibility teeters in the land of opinion. Groupware, however, stores lengthy dialogs—the assertion of opinion, the challenge of facts, the defending of positions, and an eventual building of trust and refinement of thesis. Groupware guarantees no answers, but the process induces consensus and shared comprehension.

Knowledge is, after all, a messy business. Complexity theory and quantum mechanics inform us that we cannot expect to know everything, that the world and knowledge about the world constantly reconfigure and realign. A nudge here causes catastrophe there. Observation influences measurement. Skills once cherished become obsolete, facts once absolute prove incorrect, and assumptions based on anachronisms induce disaster. Search spawns knowledge itself, perhaps obviating the original question in favor of deeper meaning or understanding.

Knowledge management requires sharing, for without participation nothing is learned and nothing is taught. Knowledge, it is often said, is the only thing that grows larger than its sources. Knowledge is about knowing where to look and how to look at things. When you contemplate knowledge, it proves incredibly rich and diverse. Every time I think I know something, I find that I am wrong. The rules shift, the bases change position, and the field expands or collapses. Either way, what I knew means either nothing or something else. Only through constant dialog, through the management of my personal knowledge, do I remain a valuable asset to my organization. And organizations remain only as viable and vibrant as their constantly evolving knowledge bases.

And in this seeming mire of unmanageable contradiction, tools emerge to help manage the rush of change. Technology in many ways drives the change. Computers designed to track populations became communication vehicles that allow college students to simultaneously draft short stories, research an ecology paper, and send e-mail to their folks. Technology changes the frameworks and the assumptions; it does it so fast that only technology can attempt to keep pace. We cannot always find a local mentor to impart answers, but somewhere in cyberspace, voices engage our inquiries, and the dialogue that ensues generates knowledge visible beyond the participants. Tools deliver fact and opinion to intended participants as well as wanderers that pursue new methods to engage their curiosity.

Tooling Up for Knowledge

As with most conceptual leaps, new technologies sprout to address various perceived opportunities to automate knowledge management. Several classes of tools have evolved to support knowledge management. Knowledge codification tools, like expert systems or indexed Web pages, transform tacit knowledge into explicit artifact. Knowledge transfer tools focus on how knowledge is shared, built, and enhanced within an organization. Finally, knowledge generation tools explore how machines aid people in the generation of ideas or actually generate new knowledge elements without human assistance.

Tools reveal the issues of personal knowledge and organizational knowledge. Personal knowledge tools enhance an individual's ability to gain and retain knowledge; organization-level tools derive from requirements to share and distribute knowledge among a population. Some tools may take on both characteristics.

If we take a competitive intelligence scenario, a document scanner and optical character recognition (OCR) software support both personal and organization purposes. On the personal level, someone may scan documents that enhance their knowledge of the business, such as trade journal articles that describe terms and technologies in a general way. The same scanner and OCR software may then capture articles specifically about competition, articles that describe product quality, industry metrics gathered by third parties, or interviews by corporate officers.

Of course, a scanner turns out to be rather ubiquitous across many problem spaces. Destination decides purpose. Personal information may end up as a file or an entry in a local database. Shared corporate knowledge assets may migrate to a Lotus Domino server, fully indexed and available to any networked knowledge seeker. In fact the shared document may have other knowledge tools applied, such as intelligent agents programmed to look specifically for the kind of information in the document—or it may be enhanced by discussions about the relevancy or value of the document.

Knowledge placed in digital form on the network may come to represent both codified knowledge and knowledge to transfer. Web-based documents may link to lessons learned that inspire statements or structure. It may also include links to discussion groups for continuous learning or clarification, or links to on-line training technology that enhances basic text and graphics with video, animation, and sound. Expert systems and other AI technologies often codify knowledge. Many organizations' structured knowledge coexists with loose amalgamations of digital artifacts easily accessed and sifted by search engines.

Sometimes tools may be more traditional than electronic. Posters, newsletters, and meetings still prove effective as knowledge transfer tools, though groupware, Web browsers, and e-mail slowly replace paper-based communiqués as the favored medium. All people demonstrate unique world views and individual learning styles. Too high a concentration on electronic media may make it difficult to communicate with the technology-aversive colleague or the over-worked executive who barely makes it through fifty daily e-mails, leaving no time to scavenge the network for useful tidbits of knowl-edge to assimilate.

Knowledge generation tools are the most difficult to describe because they are tools imbued with algorithms that combine common elements in unique ways. Knowledge generation tools help trigger ideas and support brainstorming.

In a nation of tinkerers, knowledge management inevitably mani-fests in tools. We do not form myths easily, songs do not recall our exploits, and our graffiti has deteriorated into personal edification rather than a reflection of cultural knowledge. Within Novell and Solaris servers, we find new homes for coffee klatches too pushed for time to meet, for hallway conversations in rooms of cubicles that trade space for environment, and for lunchroom conversations among people forced by deadline and discipline to eat a solitary lunch at their desk.

Automation often seeks to eliminate people from the work equa-tion. *Employee elimination leads to higher productivity*, states the motto of many organizations. It is the workers, however, that form the knowledge base of an organization, and thus establish its baseline for adaptability. If the workers leave, the factory is only as long lived as demand for its current product or process. It has no ability to retool, no ability to change. Knowledge management software engages people in process, and if they should leave an organization, some bits of opinion, knowledge, and character remain in knowledge repositories for those that follow.

Computers cache both structured and messy forms of knowl-edge with equal acuity. Structured knowledge requires intense cod-dling, but tools and techniques abound. Messy knowledge has spawned its own industry for capturing, documenting, distributing, retaining, validating, and enhancing knowledge in whatever digital form one chooses.

A Final Bit of Knowledge

Knowledge management seeks boundaries where domains connect and cross-fertilize. The edge of chaos, in biology, physics, politics, or knowledge generates unique interactions and creative combinations. Bayseian logic, uncertainty principles, fuzzy logic, and neural nets apply fuzziness to expert systems, but these techniques only define how closely a particular fact fits in a given circumstance. The fact remains a fact, firmly tied to the domain. Uncertainty applies context, but only within the most narrow of definitions. Knowledge management relishes fuzziness.

In day-to-day terms, new knowledge arises from the intersection of companies slapped together by merger or acquisition, or at discipline boundaries where computing, for instance, fades into biology. New knowledge arises from organizational change or from changes in technology that cause an enterprise to reevaluate its products or processes, and through that reevaluation, define new relationships and new meanings.

Cycles of innovation balance people and organizations on the edge between stagnation and anarchy. Individual creativity propels organizational invention. A structural engineer, unsatisfied with the latest mechanical engineering journals, may find innovative solutions in the study of bones or beaks.

Knowledge expresses the delicate and personal, the durable and public. Some wear it like loud clothing, making sure that everyone knows they have a considerable amount, but that it is to be doled out in appropriate dollops as occasion demands. Others appear drab, but hide great fortunes beneath a shy demeanor. Their knowledge is personal for reasons of pain or pride, insecurity, or instability. We try to tease knowledge out and force it into logic, but many times the knowledge resists attempts to trap it and confine it along a single dimension; other times it mutates so quickly that snapshots record only fleeting essence, not substance.

Knowledge management attempts to seize knowledge along other vectors. It attempts to facilitate dialog, capture notes, and document opinion. It attempts to position its tools quietly beneath conversations, like stones in a slow running creek. Over time, conversations, like stones, arrange themselves in a way that reflects the character of the currents. And if we look closely enough, we will always find something to learn from what has come before.

REDISCOVERING HUMAN INTELLIGENCE

Although I am still a knowledge engineer, most of 1995 was spent implementing knowledge objects rather than intelligent objects. I capture snippets of thought, fragments of sound, bits of photograph, and other artifacts and make them easy to retrieve. I work with systems that allow people to communicate with each other without regard for time or place. I have moved from writing structured rules to capturing the unstructured and random. Not only do I capture streams of consciousness much as they happen, I encourage the ramblings by bringing groupware to the desktop.

Like most emerging technologies, Groupware proves hard to pin down in its amorphous and evolving totality. In its simplest form, groupware allows people to exchange ideas in different places, at different times, and it also helps facilitate people working group-oriented tasks in the same location at the same time. Groupware is about the raw exchange of data between people. It captures random thoughts, poorly formed questions, brilliant responses—dialogs of all densities, lengths, values, and qualities.

Because of its nature, groupware needs objects and objects equally need groupware. Groupware needs objects because it attempts to put the random into order. Questions carry responses; annotations to a word processing object exist as an object layer about the basic document. Video and sound and images all reside and interact best when represented as objects.

And object-oriented programming needs groupware because the search, retrieval, and collaboration on objects and methods is one of the areas that remains to fulfill the OO dream. Although we can share and collaborate on objects, we often do not, because we cannot find what we are looking for, or have no way of connecting with the author of the object.

Conceptually, groupware solves that problem. A browser with a directory connection could connect a programmer with the originator of a class. The person need not be at the same company. Any number of methods could be used for the connection. An ISDN connection could establish a video link, with the browser defined as a shared application. A posting to the originator's most frequently visited newsgroup could begin a virtual dialog. In its most simple state, the system could generate an e-mail to the original author.

Groupware connects people in a variety of ways, but at the core, the data stored in groupware will be objects that must know how to cooperate with other objects, and how to divulge their enlightening properties.

Groupware Defined

Groupware is nearly as slippery to define as AI. Groupware includes a broad range of products from e-mail to discussion databases, to shared screen applications, and group writing tools. All the various incarnations of groupware share one common element: they act as a technology conduit for the exchange of ideas between people.

Projection screens and whiteboards that turn traditional dry erase markers into input devices predominate the same-time, same-place applications. Group decision support applications, such as Group Systems V from Ventana Systems, help facilitate meetings by capturing group brainstorming sessions and allowing attendees to categorize, rate, and vote on various ideas.

Same time, different place is perhaps the most exciting and useful of the applications. This category of software includes group-editing systems for the geographically dispersed to work on a shared document. Desktop video with application sharing puts personality, facial expression, and gesture back into the conference call, adding to a sense of camaraderie with collaborators. Once one of the most implemented technologies is remote control or screen sharing, like Farallon Corporation's Timbuktu, which allows people to see and control the computers of peers on the network, no matter where they may reside physically.

Lotus Notes dominates the corporate discussion database arena with excellent tools for asynchronous communications, while Internet newsgroups monopolize conversation on the Net. With tools like Notes and Internet newsgroups, people can collaborate not only between sites, but without regard to time. Enter a response or a question and when you arrive at work the next morning, your colleagues in London or Australia are likely to have checked in with their two-cents (or shillings) worth.

All of these applications are excellent ways to collaborate on everything from classes structures to method coding. If you have a development team in San Diego and another one in San Antonio, faxes and telephone calls are a poor substitute for shared screens and asynchronous conversations. Everyone can share ideas, work issues, and tweak code through direct interaction, before they commit the class or method to the repository.

Although groupware has its applications for object software development, this is a section about AI. Groupware is challenging AI's role for knowledge capture, retention, and distribution, and it is the media-rich object environments that make it possible.

Groupware and AI

Artificial intelligence is about structure and logic. Knowledge is dissected into very small pieces, then remapped into a language, and reconstructed, rule by rule, knowledge base by knowledge base. AI is replete with objects. A hypothesis, a single condition, or a single conclusion all represent instances of objects. Objects, as I have stated many times in these pages, are the things AI applications reason about.

Objects in any groupware system are raw, dense, obtuse, and obscure. Objects in groupware are the things reasoned about in groupware. Groupware—with the exception of agents, which I will return to in a moment—uses human rather than machine intelligence. In an AI system the values associated with objects are concise and short: strings, numbers, and Boolean values. Groupware objects capture morsels of thought, presentations, splashes of video or sound, charts, or a hand-drawn sketch in the abstract data types we tout as the power of objects.

AI concerns itself with exhaustive truth of a restricted domain, be it computer repair or space shuttle loading. Groupware forces exploration of truth. In AI all is known, at least at the moment a system goes into product. The boundaries of knowledge are strictly guarded, else the system will fail.

Groupware probes the edges of knowledge, using experts as guides and mentors. Rather than capture bits of an expert in the confines of rules, groupware passes on the legacy of the expert with dialog. Rather than teaching software, the organization learns through interactions. Sometimes the content may not be as important as the thought process related by the experts involved. A person may solve another problem by analogy from the discussion threads and the fits and starts. The questions are often more important in groupware than the answers.

In an expert system only a small number of questions can be asked or managed. Any question outside the domain fails to resolve or turns out with a ridiculous answer, like the automobile expert system answering questions about a person with measles. When the symptoms were entered, the expert system suggests stripping and repainting because the "person" was suffering from rust.

AI does have its place within groupware. As filters for the overwhelming variety of information on the Web, newsgroups, and Lotus Notes databases, intelligent agents present people with a more concise picture of cyberspace. AI whittles away at the expanse of data on the Net.

The very act of narrowing the window, though, demonstrates the difficulties with current AI. An agent cannot make a leap of faith or a connection to a thing not explicitly coded. A Web crawler may search all connections on each page it encounters. It cannot fathom the meaning of a URL or the free text of a Web page to determine its relevance. It is all or some or nothing.

The some is the problem. AI cannot intuit the connection between structural spacecraft design and animal physiology. A person might find the next way to make lighter spacecraft by a happenstance encounter with avian bone structure. An AI searching and filtering would never present the avian data given the usual strict definitions ascribed to agent search criteria. Only a human with random, but informed curiosity, could discover both the connection and the value in the connection.

Groupware, as loose as it is compared to AI, is the knowledge trend of the 1990s. AI still fills niche roles and works with groupware for filtering (and scheduling in group schedulers), but AI is more intelligent searcher than it is advisor or repository. Groupware is quickly becoming the repository of corporate knowledge. Lotus Notes databases, internal Newsgroup servers, and other technologies store increasing amounts of intellectual capital. And now, and in the future, much of that knowledge will be stored in the raw, in objects that facilitate search, object compositions, and interaction.

The Object of Groupware

Objects will prove to be the best way to manage the complex world of knowledge being stored on various media throughout an organization. Video, sound, and other document components will eventually replace the already arcane markup language of the Web. Data will remain data, but the richer data types will provide it predigested and interactive. It will know about itself and about its relationships to other things. Searches will be more confined and less random.

Our repositories of objects will not be object stores, but knowledge stores. Some objects will have their own intelligence, acting much as today's monolithic expert systems do. They will solve problems, provide advice, and search for things. Other objects will store bits of human intelligence in raw form. Their methods will be concerned with video playback, text to speech, or various kinds of display. The contents of the raw knowledge objects will be the history, the lore, the anecdotes and the speeches, crude pictures, and well-executed drawings.

Our encounters with knowledge objects will generate new objects that retain our thought patterns, our curiosities, and our opinions. And with objects we will be able to connect histories and versions, making the path of creation explicit. Knowledge need not fit the constraints of Prolog or CLIPS or OPS5. I may learn more from a few minutes in a newsgroup than I do reading the dry logic of an expert-system application.

Groupware encourages people to interact. Virtual encounters may not come with hot coffee or warm handshakes, but they will be much more personal and responsive than e-mail. People will build relationships with each other, and retain those relationships as object links to newsgroups, e-mail, or video conferencing connections. A point and a click will take you from concept to fact to contact.

We so often focus on the details that it is difficult to remember that our lives and our businesses are made largely from human contact. Groupware is no panacea for our lack of communication, but it isn't another alienating technology like voice mail either. In my experience people engage in the groupware environment because of need or interest, and that is at least a starting point.

Amid all of our technological solutions to perceived human dilemmas, a technology that rediscovers human intelligence is a welcome addition to any analyst's box of tricks.

OO-Related Newsgroups

If you want to start interacting with other OO aficionados, here is a list of Internet newsgroups related to object-oriented subjects.

comp.lang.smalltalk

comp.lang.c++

comp.lang.clos

gnu.smalltalk.bug

comp.lang.eiffel

comp.lang.objective-c

comp.databases.object

comp.object

comp.object.logic

comp.ai.shells

comp.groupware

comp.groupware.lotus-notes.misc

comp.sys.mac.oop.misc

comp.os.os2.programmer.oop

AFTERWORD

After re-reading all of my articles from the last several years—which were compiled for this book—I realize that the industry for intelligent objects exists with huge potential, but little leadership. The community has vacillated from suppliers bent on selling proprietary reasoning engines, to selling their own cross-platform development tools, to selling their inference engines as business process reengineering tools. Most recently older tools, once the pride of C++, are now showing up as Java applets, ready for corporate Intranets.

At the 1997 Object World conference in San Francisco, not one AI company attended. Object World used to be a no-brainer for AI companies. Many were in the Bay Area and they all had objects, at least frames, to represent information. Perhaps this is a blip or a reflection on the show organizer and not the technology, but it was very strange covering a show that at one point took me two days of meetings just to see the AI products. In 1997 only stalwart Franz, Inc. was showing anything remotely like AI—their Franz Common LISP.

Miller Freeman's Software Develop '98 offered some hope, as Neuron Data, Ilog, and Platinum dusted off their wares and showed both development tools and the intelligent products. Gone are the days of vapid idealization about AI. The same tools now focus on solving business problems or representing business rules on the Web. Another trait at all of these companies, though, is the lack of product evolution. Mergers have transformed packaging; language preferences have moved from C to C++ and now to Java. But the basic engines are the same. Perhaps there's a little cleaner connectivity to databases, better APIs, or a different platform, but from the reasoning standpoint, they're the same—1980's inference engines wrapped in a new veneer.

Many organizations continue research, including several governments. I saw a presentation recently on one of DARPA's latest endeavors, high performance knowledge bases. Although the idea of a knowledge base, using the principles of database technology, was a new twist moving toward a common knowledge interface, what DARPA plans on storing in this new representation are the same axioms of knowledge DARPA projects have stored for decades: Smallish bits of military description translated from English into predicate calculus so the machine can reason in a way that we reason, after we stop reasoning and think so hard our wisdom spills out in a form most humans are unable to read. The inference mechanisms are the same. The thinking about thinking has not moved forward, not at least in implementation. We have not seen real reasoning software, perhaps not because our research is flawed, but because our questions are too parochial.

Our questions always start with reason, even if the mind of a child is incapable of reason. Children absorb and connect, but early in their development they cannot argue or form logical inferences. The first order of business is to bring AI down to a more primitive level, to a level where the world is much less explicit. My children learned about heat from a stovetop by violating a rule about not touching the stove. No amount of information about the heat of the stove was going to relate heat to them the way the heat did. No amount of logical discussion and predicate calculus describing the nature of heat was going to deter them from touching the stove. Only the experience of heat itself could teach the lesson in the end. And it was the contradiction of logic that led to the permanent storage and respect for the original rule. Not a common principle in AI research.

This small story brings up another point about our search for connecting silicon logic and human reasoning. Most of our knowledge is wrapped in multisensory experience. Computers don't have the same sense of sense that we have. We should not expect software to relate to our world or our sensibilities if it does not exist in our world.

The very nature of our intellect is derived from evolutionary pressures perceived by our senses and thus inextricably connected to them. The computer's sensory input will not come from rods or cones, fingertips or malleus, incus, stapes, or cochlea. The computer will learn about its world through RS-232, USB, and SCSI inputs, scanners and microphones, digital cameras, and modems and telephones. The discontinuity of experience is enough to differentiate our creations from use as much as we are discontinuous in experience with dogs and their 256 gray-scale vision and more acute hearing. No amount of logic will bridge the gap of experience and input.

The idea that logic alone informs our consciousness is an absurd conjecture. This statement does not invalidate a mechanistic view of consciousness or an inability to create consciousness in a non-organic manner, but simply that we constrain both ourselves and our creations too narrowly, that non-deterministic processes govern much of our behavior. Wedding artificial intelligence to logic straight-jackets software into deterministic behavior and therefore denies it any chance of evolution that would lead to a unique software-hardware consciousness.

The next generation of AI researchers should look toward systems that construct themselves from primitive code. Perhaps each processor, operating system, or language will generate a different set of starting conditions that will lead to a different configuration of components. The software should be provided with basic structures for self-associative memory that will absorb information and then place that information into its own context, based on other information in the system, allowing the software itself to optimize its storage, rather than relying on preconceived notions of storage built around our expectations of retrieval needs.

Self-associative memory will require dropping into a prelogic world, a world where I think most AI researchers will feel very uncomfortable. Neural network aficionados may feel a bit more at home, but they still see the world as sets of numbers and probabilities, abstracting away the organic of the mental equation. The software I'm describing will be capable of ascertaining the unique characteristics of its environment and optimizing itself for that environment.

AI needs to rethink itself along the lines of artificial life, seeking to build primitives that evolve. Artificial life simulated certain characteristics of biological systems, which resulted in basic biological behavior, but I have seen little progress in moving artificial life beyond its basics.

Our next attempts need to move away from our vision of intelligence, imbuing software with learning ability tied to internal motiva-
tions. For in the end, our evolutionary discretion comes from our
motivation to survive and procreate, a motivation unknown to software. We must provide simple tools and simple goals and see where
these lead. As I wrote earlier in the book, artificial intelligence may
turn out to be something intelligent, but it may turn out to be intelligent only within its own framework. We use these tools, but they
are not connected directly to our consciousness. What will it mean
to an evolving software entity that it has a high-bandwidth connection to the Internet?. We cannot imagine and therefore cannot pre-
sume how the intelligence will use its senses. We need to provide
the goal and the infrastructure and see how, or if, our software can
find a more unique way to use this sense than evolve into a glorified
search engine.

And with the mass of data available in and around computers, we
should find ways that these systems can reflect on their own knowledge. Most AI systems are horrible at learning. Knowledge-based systems require huge amounts of overhead when the world shifts.
People must rewrite their rules and hone their interfaces. From the
practical standpoint, expert systems are fine business tools and the
overhead required to maintain them is the cost of doing business.
But based on the goals of AI's early champions, they are evolutionary
dead ends; they are the Neanderthals of AI, branching off the evolutionary tree, ripe in their own way, but incapable of contributing
material to the future.

Learning and adaptation are essential. Reflection would allow AI
systems to find new patterns in their stored memories and associate
things, perhaps in a way meaningful to them, but meaningless to us.
Again the context. We impose our framework on something that has
a different framework and expect it to produce a result that is meaningful in our framework. That is the trap of expert systems and why
they will never grow beyond their current state. AI is not beyond our
technology, we are just too snared by our own framework, assuming
ourselves the perfection of logic, all the while starring at a device
more logical, concise, and repeatable in its answers than any human
being. And rather than provide that device with software that suits its
framework, we impose ours, immediately limiting the device to a
poor emulation of something we barely understand.

So we much focus on how to think like the device rather than
have the device think like us. And with our wonderful imaginations,

too often cluttered with ego to be truly useful, we can think like a machine. Danny Hillis reinvented the computer as a massively parallel device, perhaps one more capable of learning and acting intelligent than single processors on desktops, but the need to think like his machine eluded most programmers. The Connection Machine forced programmers to think like the machine, which Hillis could do, but few others found the proper motivation. Some of these wonderful devices have been sold for as little as $500 to private collectors.

Despite faster computers, and that is what Moore's law fanatics look for, it is the software that matters, not the speed of the computer. The right software will work, albeit slowly, even on an Intel 286. It is not the connections or circuits in the CPU, but the information connections stored in memory that will differentiate stupidity from brilliance, in much the same way it does in people. Wisdom and learning are not evaluated by the rotundness of our skulls, but the rhetoric of our lips. In the AI community, we measure things in logical inferences per second, not in instructions per second. But one leads to the other and neither leads to intelligence.

In business process reengineering we find the same human fallacy. We improve processes and we make organizations work faster and harder, most often ignoring the question of the value of the task, only gauging its efficiency, not its meaning. The entire organization might be more efficient if we just stopped doing certain things or if we did them completely differently, but as adaptable as we are, we are still in our frameworks and look at our solutions from the same frameworks and thus find better ways of doing the same things rather than reinventing the processes entirely.

So the faster machine leads to faster idiot savants. To paraphrase the now cliched Clinton campaign slogan: It's the software stupid. We think we know how machines should think so we throw more hardware at the solution, hoping, as Doug Lenat and his team at Cycorp perhaps still believe, that enough axioms and enough inference methods will create the context and the machine will discover its intelligence.

But CYC is a machine of predicate calculus. Rather than ask our machines to understand in our artificial language of mathematics, perhaps we should ask agents and agencies—or as Marvin Minksy sees them, "societies of mind"—to find some way to understand us and contribute to our understanding by adding their unique perspective. We can provide these agencies with inputs of logic or image, sound, or word and ask them a question and then see how they decide best to use what we provide. We should also give them the tools to explore their own world, within their own framework, the ways of swapping code or searching the Net. And then rather than remember everything as we have taught it, allow them to decide what is important and not important, saving only the relevant and reorganizing what is saved into a private construct, optimized for their framework.

We have no need to understand their internal storage methods, only their outputs. We study our own brains so that we might repair them or recreate them. The former is a noble goal, the latter less than necessary if we pursue the arguments presented here. We do not have the same raw materials as nature, and therefore the intelligence we create will be different. We should spend our time speculating on how to better make that environment conducive to intelligence than trying to impose our bio-mechanical frailties on it.

If I make a statement to a reader, a person sitting next to me on a plane, or a person chatting with me over the Net, I do not care what associations result from my statements, except as those associations manifest themselves as outputs from the other person. The contemplated words or phrases, gestures, or expressions that remain unexpressed have no bearing on the conversation or me. Personal knowledge, fear, memory, or loves do not constrain people from conversing (except in the most dysfunctional cases). We pass information back and forth; where my brain stores this information or what auxiliary set of responses is triggered has no bearing on the intellectual content of the dialog except as it enhances or modifies the external representation of those responses in words or visual queues.

Of course, humans, at some level, have a basic set of mechanisms we share for laying down and retrieving knowledge, but these mechanisms in no way manifest themselves except when we explicitly study them for the sake of understanding the phenomenon itself.

So why do we continue to constrain our software to artificial representations of internal processes we clearly do not understand ourselves? We attach an attribute, such as logic, and drill deeply into its importance for understanding, and then box ourselves into our own logic, failing to see that no matter how much logic we use, we will never be able to explain the color blue to a computer. Even if we outfit our hardware with cameras and point them at a blue we know and love, the computer will have no context for the color and see only digital splashes that fit a wholly different framework of understanding.

Our ability to appreciate blue is deeply and uniquely connected to our humanity. It is unimportant if an artificial intelligence is capable of seeing blue the way we see it, but that is what we expect when we set a goal for teaching an AI to read a newspaper—we expect it to understand time and color, feeling, and circumstance the way we do. It is more important, perhaps, that we let our software figure out for itself what the world means to it in its unique silicon immobility. As our neurons matured from suprapharyngeal ganglia to complex synapses capable of not only discerning blue from red, but coming to love a particular shade of blue, we should allow our software to learn what its own world means in its own context, and allow it to add that unique perspective to our own. Perhaps rather than teach software to be as mundane as we are, we should let it be what it will be—allowing it to love its own version of something as meaningful to us as a blue sky over San Francisco Bay on a cool May evening.

As I wrote in the introduction to this book many months ago, *there are many ways to program*. Creating objects of limited intelligence can be done with today's tools and techniques. Creating objects that find their own path will require shifting our thoughts away from ourselves toward our creations, and that is perhaps what was the intention of AI research all along.

INTELLIGENT OBJECT
BUYERS GUIDE

Amzi Logic Server and WebLS

Amzi! inc.
5861 Greentree Road
Lebannon, OH 45036
Telephone: 513-425-8050
Fax: 513-425-8025
E-mail: info@amzi.com
WWW: http://www.amzi.com
Platforms: Microsoft Windows
Price: The Professional Edition is $598 and includes 16- and
               32-bit tools and libraries and an unlimited royalty-free
               runtime. The Personal Edition is $298 and is limited to
               non-commercial distribution only. The 16-bit Profes-
               sional Edition is $298, but includes 16-bit libraries, and
               an unlimited royalty free runtime. The Amzi! Logic
               Server supports logic rules encapsulated in objects
               and/or logic rules that reason over objects. It is a
               Prolog (Logic Base) engine encapsulated in a DLL that
               can be both embedded in other applications and
               extended to access external information. C++ pro-
               grams receive a Logic Server class, Delphi program-
               mers use a Delphi Component, and Visual Basic
               programmers use a set of cover functions. The native
               API is available directly for all other host environ-
               ments, such as Smalltalk.

The Logic Server can be extended to reason over other objects. One example is the provided ODBC connection that allows records in ODBC databases to be reasoned over directly by Prolog code. This same mechanism can be used to extend the Logic Server to reason over input devices such as temperature or pressure gauges in a manufacturing process, or over hardware configuration settings.

Amzi recently released WebLS to bring the basic capabilities of their Logic Server to the Web environment.

GBB

Blackboard Technology Group
401 Main Street
Amherst, MA 01002
Telephone: 800-577-8990
              413-256-8990
Fax: 413-256-3179
E-mail: info@bbtech.com
WWW: http://www.bbtech.com
Platforms: Macintosh, Windows 3.1, Windows 95, Windows NT, and Unix machines from Sun, Digital, Hewlett-Packard, IBM, and Silicon Graphics.
Price: $5,000 and up

GBB is the leading commercial implementation of the blackboard architecture, known colloquially as groupware for applications. GBB implements blackboards in CLOS LISP structures with robust mechanisms for the exchange of information between individual software agents.

With GBB, teams of experts and programmers can develop knowledge sources asynchronously, leading to a modular, evolutionary style of development. Although GBB is LISP-based, it can integrate knowledge sources from a variety of programming languages and does not constrain knowledge representation to a single style. Any knowledge source that used the GBB interfaces can share information with GBB.

Blackboard Technology group also sells ChalkBox for GUI development and NetGBB for distributed blackboards.

ART*Enterprise

Brightware, Inc.
350 Ignacio Blvd., Suite 100
Novato, CA 94949
Telephone   415-884-4774
Fax   415-884-4740
E-mail   info@brightware.com
WWW   http://www.brightware.com
Platforms: Windows 3.1, Windows95, Windows NT, Solaris, HP-UX,
              and AIX.
Price: $8,000 and up

ART*Enterprise is a high-end tool for the integration of knowledge elements with existing procedural code and databases. Art implements the RETE algorithm for rule processing and includes strong interfaces for RDBMS integration with Oracle, Synapses, and SQLServer. Other databases use the generic ODBC interface.

Several programming styles are included with ART*Enterprise, including object-oriented programming, rules, case-based reasoning, procedural programming, and hypothetical reasoning with consistency management. All of these paradigms are incorporated into ARTScript, which uses incremental compilation and runtime dynamic code generation.

ART*Enterprise programming is supported by several 4GL tools, including a screen painter, forms generator, object browser, and data integrator. ART*Enterprise also supports debugging through its source-level debugger and includes a System Reuse Manager for searching across projects for class libraries.

ART*Enterprise also supports World Wide Web services through TCP/IP sockets for transmitting HTTP to and from the Web/ART*Enterprise server, an HTTP Protocol handler for converting incoming HTTP to underlying ART*Enterprise request objects, and a merge facility for merging ART*Enterprise responses with HTML, Java, or other Web GUI elements.

Goldworks III

Gold Hills, Inc.
36 Arlington Road
Chestnut Hill, MA 02167
Telephone: 617-621-3300
Fax: 617-621-0656
E-mail: info@goldhill-inc.com
WWW: http://www.goldhill-inc.com/
Platforms: Windows 3.1 with WIN32s 1.15+ and Windows NT,
              and compatible with OS/2 3.0 withWIN32s 1.15+.

Goldworks III beefs up its LISP-based expert-system environment to
include a improved Foreign Function Interface for integration of
external information sources and support for DDE. Goldworks III
also includes the complete GCLISP 5.0 environment.

Frames, multiple inheritance, multi-directional rules, and rules
sets are standard features within Goldworks. The tool also includes
an extensive graphic capability for authoring customer graphical
interfaces that dynamically change based on values within the runtime environment. CLOS objects can be easily integrated into the
GoldWorks III's frames and rules.

Although developed in LISP, Goldworks III includes runtime modules and source-code protection that lock end users out of the development environment. Goldworks III also support SQL integration
through the Golden Connection/SQL, which connects to databases
that support Microsoft's ODBC standard.

Eclipse, Rete ++, The Easy Reasoner, Help!CPR

The Haley Enterprise, Inc.
413 Orchard Street
Sewickley, PA 15143
Telephone: 800-233-2622
            412-741-6420
Fax: 412-741-6457
E-mail: info@haley.com
WWW: http://www.haley.com
Platforms: Windows, OS/2, various Unix, DOS, Macintosh, MVS
            and Tandem.
Price: $499 and up, depending on product and features.

The Haley Enterprise has consciously not attacked the high end of the OO AI market with a fully integrated set of tools that are as much GUI-building environments for client/server applications as they are AI tools. Instead, Haley points its suite of products at the C, C++, and Visual Basic developer who needs to incorporate reasoning into their application. This strategy reflects itself in some of the fastest reasoning code on the market.

Eclipse and RETE++ provide the basic class libraries and other code to integrate CLIPS/OPS-based rules into C++. Unlike other tools that use proprietary frames for knowledge representation, these products use standard rules and C++. In addition, Eclipse is significantly more true to early designs of the RETE algorithm by retaining backward chaining, truth maintenance, and nested representation not found in later commercial implementations of RETE based on NASA's CLIPS code.

In addition to Eclipse and Rete++, The Haley Enterprise also sells The Easy Reasoner that integrates with RETE++ to provide full case-based reasoning (CBR) to C++ applications. The Easy Reasoner retrieves information from databases as a comparison to a case currently in memory. It will also mine databases for their conceptual structure. Like other CBR products, The Easy Reasoner learns from additions to its case library, circumventing the need to manage individual rules and their relationships.

Haley has recently extended The Easy Reasoner's CBR technology into a product called Help!CPR, which provides help desk reasoning tools in the form of a C++ class library.

This set of tools gives programmers powerful tools for integrating reasoning into standard code without the need to learn complex environments or maintain information in proprietary formats. The integration with C++ makes RETE++ and its associated tools the best choice for low overhead reasoning in an OOP application.

KnowledgeWorks

Harlequin Inc.
301 Ravenswood Ave, Suite 100
Menlo Park, CA 94025
Telephone: 415-833-0400
Fax: 415833-4111
E-mail: web@harlequin.com
WWW: http://www.harlequin.com
Platforms: Available on a wide range of Unix workstations, including: DEC Alpha, OSF/1; DEC MIPS, Ultrix; Sun SPARC, SunOS; Sun SPARC, Solaris; SGI MIPS, IRIX; IBM RS6000, AIX; and HP PA 9000/700, HP-UX.
Price: LispWorks environment ($4,500 single-user seat) plus KnowledgeWorks ($1,500 single-user seat).

Harlequin is primarily known for its LISP products, which include rule-based capabilities in its KnowledgeWorks. KnowledgeWorks adds mixin capabilities to standard CLOS for its knowledge representation. Mixin enables rules to pattern match against the CLOS objects. Both forward and backward chaining are supported within the rule base.

Contexts help organize KnowledgeWorks rule sets into logical subdomains. This helps developers manage knowledge and evoke different domains as required by the facts in memory.

Forward chaining logic is stored in OPS-based syntax while backward chaining is written in Prolog. Both LISP and Edinburgh style syntax is available for backward-chained rules.

KnowledgeWorks is built atop Harlequin's LispWorks product and integrates LispWorks features like database interfacing.

Ilog Rules

Ilog
2005 Landings Drive
Mountain View, CA 94043
Telephone: 800-367-4564
Fax: 415-390-0946
E-Mail: info@ilog.com
WWW: http://www.ilog.com
Platforms: Various Unix, OS/2, Windows, Windows NT . . . and
             Windows 95.
Price: Windows ($6,500), UNIX, OS/2 ($10,000)

Like RETE++ from The Haley Enterprise, Ilog's Ilog Rules uses native C++ objects in conjunction with the RETE algorithm to provide rapid reasoning integration with existing code. Ilog Rules knowledge is compiled into a C++ class library that easily integrates with applications though a simple API. The evaluation of C++ expressions is supported in both the condition and action parts of a rules, enforcing the integration of the rules into the overall application object model.

Advanced functions of Ilog Rules include a Truth Maintenance System (TMS) as well as counting, NOT, and EXIST primitives.

Ilog rules integrates with other Ilog C++ products including ILOG Views GUI builder, ILOG DB Link for RDBMS access, ILOG Server for simplified application integration, ILOG Broker for distributed object computing, ILOG Solver for business resource optimization, ILOG Schedule for scheduling, and ILOG Talk for fast prototyping.

PowerModel, KappaPC

IntelliCorp
1975 El Camino Real West, Suite 101
Mountain View, CA 94040-2216
Telephone: 650-965-5500
Fax: 650-965-5647
E-mail: sales@intellicorp.com
WWW: http://www.intellicorp.com
Platforms: Windows 3.1, Windows NT, OS/2 2.1
Price: $12,990 and up depending on options

IntelliCorp has grown from its LISP-based roots in the Knowledge Engineering Environment (KEE) to C and PowerModel, previously known as Kappa Professional. PowerModel is an integrated environment for building complete applications. PowerModel is built in ANSI C with APIs and interfaces for including external code and for embedded PowerModel applications within other applications.

IntelliCorp has moved away from the pure AI area and now positions PowerModel as an integrated tool in its ModelWorks product line. Other tools in this line include LiveModel, which is a CASE tool built on PowerModel. LiveModel combines sophisticated modeling tools with code generation for a complete environment that moves from CASE models to executable code.

Third party developers and consultants can extend LiveModel by building tool sets called ModelBridge Solutions. The first two Model-Bridge solutions support C++, and TCSI's OSP. The C++ bridge supports the development of objects and relationships with the generation of C++ code and header files directly from the models. OSP support included modeling distributed objects and their domains. A third ModelBridge solution is available for SAP R/3. R/3 support helps implementers of the SAP product simulate their business engineering decisions prior to implementation.

IntelliCorp also continues to sell and support the object-oriented KappaPC for smaller expert systems targeted for desktop deployment.

AionDS 8.0

Platinum Technology Inc.
1815 South Meyers Road
Oakbrook Terrace, IL 60181-5241
Telephone: 800-442-6861
             708-620-5000
Fax: 708-691-0710
E-mail: techsup@platinum.com
WWW: http://www.platinum.com
Platforms: Windows 3.X, Windows NT, Windows 95, OS/2, HP/UX,
             AIX, Solaris, MVS, CICS and IMS.

Like other integrated AI environments, AionDS offers rules, GUIs, and database integration in the context of a proprietary object environment. AionDS supports mixed mode rule and object development through an extensive graphical development environment.

AionDS has been around for a while and has evolved less dramatically than some others, but its length of service retains some valuable legacy integration tools that allow it to import object definitions directly from COBOL or PL/1 applications. It also continues to support both MVS and VM on IBM mainframe computers. AionDS also includes strong database integration elements and is the only product I know of that integrates with third party CASE environments.

AionDS, however, has not been abandoned even after mergers that first generated Trinzic Corporation, which later merged with software giant Platinum Technology. In the 7.0 version of AionDS class libraries will be introduced as modular knowledge repositories. Other enhancements include an Extended FPL API, OLE control integration, Informix Database support, and various GUI enhancements like multi-column list box controls and extended font and color support.

M4

Teknowledge Corporation
1810 Embarcadero Road
Palo Alto, CA 94303
Telephone: 650-424-0500
WWW: http://www.teknowlege.com
Platforms: Windows
Price: $995 and up

M4 is derived from one of the original expert system products, M1. M4 still retains some of its LISP roots, but is not a fully callable library that can be linked to a variety of Windows development environments, including Visual Basic, Visual C++, and Toolbook. M4 can be linked to executables or called as DLL. Unlike some more memory intensive environments, DOS applications can run on as little as 512K and Windows applications require only 4MB of RAM.

The heritage of M4 is one of backward chaining, but this modern version performs forward chaining through whenfound/whencached and procedures. Tools for basic user interfaces are included, along with internal facilities for value checking, knowledge base encryption, and explanations of inferences. Strong debugging tools, such as tracing, single-step mode, and logging help manage complex knowledge bases.

The object environment adds objects as variables using CLOS-derived proprietary object extensions. The objects extensions include definition of classes of objects, the creation of instances, inheritance of slots, values, and methods, overriding of inheritance for slots, values and methods, and message passing between objects. Development takes place in simple editors and the knowledge base is stored as text.

M4 is a robust rule and object environment, but because it is aimed at embedded systems, rather than a total solution, it requires significant integration between the rule base and the user interface. The knowledge representation, however, is well tested and has been used in many expert systems. Its syntax will appeal to Prolog programmers, but it is relatively easy to pick up for the non-logic initiated. M4 shows its value as an embedded tool in a variety of potential Windows applications that may need inference, complex string manipulation and other advanced features.

Level5 Object Professional

Level Five Research
1335 Gateway Drive, Suite 2005,
Melbourne, Florida 32901
Telephone: 1-800-444-4303
             407-29-6004
Fax: 407-727-7615
E-mail: sales@l5r.com
WWW: http://www.l5r.com
Platforms: Microsoft Windows

Level5 Object, once sold as a general purpose expert-system shell, is now being targeted as an extension to Windows programming environments like Visual Basic, PowerBuilder, and Lotus Notes. Calling out from these environment to Level5 Object provides basic knowledge representation and rule execution capabilities.

Level Five Research achieves tight integration within the Windows environment by delivering Level5 Object as an OLE 2 Automation Server so it is available to any application running in Windows.

Level5 Object rules and objects are developed in a graphical environment. Rules are expressed in a very simple English-like syntax with key words easily accessible from pop-up menus. Rules designated as triggers examine incoming data streams and execute based on current data values.

The GUI building environment is both extensive and extensible. Basic GUI widgets like buttons and scrolling text fields are supplemented by multimedia extensions for sound and video. Database integration is delivered in the form of ODBC, Q&E, and parent company Information Builders' EDA/SQL.

Completed applications are delivered by the runtime Level5 Agent. Because rules are often very prized commodities in corporate espionage, knowledge bases delivered by Level5 Agent can be encrypted prior to distribution.

Prolog++/flex

Logic Programming Associates Ltd.
Studio 4, R.V.P.B.
Trinity Road, London
SW18 3SX, England UK
Telephone: +44 (0) 181 871 2016
Fax: +44 (0) 181 874 0449
E-mail: lpa@cix.compulink.co.uk
WWW: http://www.lpa.co.uk
Platforms: Windows and Macintosh.
Price: $795.00 for the Programmer Edition and $1,495.00 for
              the Developer Edition

Logic Programming Associates of the United Kingdom has extended
Prolog to include dynamic objects. Prolog++ brings objects into the
interpreted world of Prolog where, like LISP, garbage collection is
automatic and variables are type free. This creates a powerful combination that allows Prolog to reason over both standard Prolog declarations and more structure objects. Prolog++ objects include part-of
and isa-relationships.

Prolog++ objects have direct connections to the greater Prolog
environment and may include external code written in C, C++, or
Pascal. LPA Prolog also includes support for DLLs and DDE within
Windows. LPA also developed the flex expert-system shell, which
provides traditional rules, frames, and other expert-system capabilities within the Prolog++ environment.

Rule Elements and Advisor/J

Neuron Data
1310 Villa Street
Mountain View, CA 94041
Telephone: 800-876-4900
             650-528-3450
Fax: 650-943-2762
E-mail: info@neurondata.com
WWW: http://www.neurondata.com
Platforms: Microsoft Windows, Windows NT, OS/2, Macintosh over
             one dozen Unix and Digital operating systems.
Price: $6,850

Neuron Data is another AI company that moves in and out of the AI business, while retaining the same basic product line. They first entered the market with Nexpert Object, then moved toward client/server development selling the cross-platform development tools used to create Nexpert. At this point Nexpert became either an "Intelligent" or "Rule" element of the Elements suite of tools. The company most recently rewrote the Nexpert engine in Java and now sells it as Advisor/J, business rule engine for Web-based applications and other Java applications.

All of Neuron Data's rule-based tools include an extensive graphical development environment, including rule and object browsers. Pop-up menus throughout the various notebooks and editors help with navigation and syntax. The context editor sets up the initial environment and suggests initial hypothesis for backward chaining. The whole environment however is flexible and can be modified and initiated at runtime. Developers can set check points on either data or rules for debugging purposes.

Neuron Data continues to demonstrate strong leadership in the rule-bases arena while expanding their product line to include a complete set of development tools.

G2

Gensym Corporation
125 Cambridge Park Drive
Cambridge, MA 02140
Telephone: 617-547-2500
Fax: 617-547-1962
E-mail: info@gensym.com
WWW: http://www.gensym.com

G2 is an intelligent OO tool for the real-time control of processes. G2 supports OO modeling, real-time execution, rule-based and model-based reasoning, multi-threaded concurrent execution procedures, structured natural language, and interactive graphics.

Unique to G2 is the spatial representations found in its rules. Because of the process orientation, its inference engine understands things like "connected downstream." From this it reduces the search space of elements to only those that are after the current process. This is further refined to the concepts of location and proximity, which help in inventory or scheduling applications.

G2 has been used in monitoring and diagnosis, optimization, scheduling, supervisor control, and process modeling and simulation. G2 employs both event driven rules and data-seeking rules that interact with knowledge representation objects and graphic element in the user interface.

Unlike most of the tools listed here, G2 goes beyond SQL interfaces to include interfaces for standard control systems, data collectors, and simulators.

RTworks

Talarian
444 Castro Street, Suite 140
Mountain View, CA 94041
Telephone: 650-965-8050
Fax: 650-965-9077
E-mail: info@talarian.com
WWW: http://www.talarian.com

RTworks is an applications framework for building client/server applications that are based on time dependencies. You would not use RTworks for diagnosing your PC, but you may well use it for diagnosing your wide area network and its plethora of routers and switches.

RTworks consists of several modules, including those for middleware (SmartSockets), graphical user interface development (RThei), and data acquisition (RTdaq). Key to the discussion here is RTie, the rule development environment. RTie uses rules to reason about objects, classes, and the state of variables user defined procedural code. Rules can execute at a certain time or through standard forward and backward chaining.

Because RTie is designed to run in seven-by-twenty-four applications, it has the unique ability to keep running while the knowledge base is modified. Developers can send messages to a running application, which add or delete rules from a knowledge base. RTie's real-time operation has resulted in temporal reasoning elements that represent data real time from external sources.

Rules are developed in a Motif-based GUI with menus to aid in the construction of rules and results. In addition to the built-in functions, RTie comes with C/C++ libraries and interface functions for easy interaction with external applications. RTie can be incorporated as a callable function by other systems.

RTworks is a high-performance system design for real-time applications. The inclusion of RTie removes the need to rely on another reasoning engine for diagnosis or analysis. RTie processes its rules very rapidly, keeping up with the incoming stream of data with barely a bead of sweat on any of the several Sparc processors sharing in its inferencing.

The Selling Chain

Trilogy
6034 W. Courtyard Drive
Austin, TX 78730
Telephone: 512-794-5900
Fax: 512-794-8900
E-mail: info@trilogy.com
WWW: http://www.trilogy.com

Trilogy sells a number of object-oriented AI tools to assist in selling
and marketing products. They provide custom solutions to several
companies as well as market the Selling Chain, an integrated set of AI-
based tools for assisting companies in the selling and marketing of
products. The Selling Chain consists of several modules, including SC
Catalog, SC Config, SC Web, and SC Proposal.

SELECT
BIBLIOGRAPHY

The books listed here are the important sources of what I know of
AI. Certainly years of reading *PC AI*, *Object Magazine*, *AI Expert*, and
Byte have also contributed significantly to my knowledge of AI, as
did the long hours of work associated with my certificate in Intelligent Systems Engineering from the University of California, Irvine,
which was granted to me in 1989. And of course there were hours
spent in conversation with the inventors of AI and their students,
and with research professors and industrial engineers working
on projects for NASA or DARPA. The most significant book on this
list is Grant Fjermedal's *The Tomorrow Makers*. That is the book
that shifted me from Material Requirements Planning (MRP) to AI.
Reading that book inspired the possibility that science fiction was
not as much about fiction as I thought. And so for the next decade I
thought about thinking and many of those thoughts have been compiled in this book.

Agre, Philip E., and Stanley J. Rosenschein, eds. *Computational Theo-
 ries of Interaction and Agency*. The MIT Press, 1996.
Barr, Avron, and Edward Feigenbaum, eds. *The Handbook of Artifi-
 cial Intelligence*. William Kaufman, Inc., 1981.
Carrico, Michael, and John E. Girard, et al. *Building Knowledge Sys-
 tems*. McGraw-Hill Book Company, 1989.
Cizko, Gary. *Without Miracles*. The MIT Press, 1995.
Clancy, William J., and Stephen W. Smoliar, eds. *Contemplating Minds*.
 The MIT Press, 1994.

Depew, David J., and Bruce H. Weber. *Darwinism Evolving*. MIT Press, 1996.

Feigenbaum, Edward, and Pamela McCorduck, et al. *The Rise of the Expert Company*. Times Books, 1988.

Fjermedal, Grant. *The Tomorrow Makers*. Macmillan Publishing Company, 1986.

Fraser, A., H. Sloate, et al. *ECAPP: Experience With a Process Planning Tool Using Artificial Intelligence*. Autofact 90, Detroit, MI. The Engineering Society of Detroit, 1990.

Gleick, James. *Chaos*. Viking, 1987.

Goldman, Alvin I. *Readings in Philosophy and Cognitive Science*. The MIT Press, 1993.

Gould, Stephen J. *The Panda's Thumb*. Norton, 1980.

——. *Hen's Teeth and Horse's Toes*. Norton, 1983.

——. *The Flamingo's Smile*. Norton, 1985.

——. *Wonderful Life*. Norton, 1989.

——. *Bully for Brontosaurus*. Norton, 1991.

——. *Eight Little Piggies*. Norton, 1993.

——. *Dinosaur in a Haystack*. Harmony Books, 1995.

Hofstadter, Douglas. *Fluid Concepts and Creative Analogies*. Basic Books, 1995.

Hume, David. *A Treatise of Human Nature*. Penguin Books, 1969.

Irizarry-Lopez, Vilma Mil. "A Methodology For The Automatic Generation Of Process Plans In An Electronic Assembly Environment." Ph.D., Purdue University, 1989.

Kelly, Richard V. Jr. *Practical Knowledge Engineering*. Digital Press, 1991.

Kim, Won. *Introduction to Object-Oriented Databases*. MIT Press. 1990.

Kusiak, A. *Intelligent Manufacturing Systems*. Prentice Hall, 1990.

Lakoff, George. *Women, Fire and Other Dangerous Things*. The University of Chicago Press, 1987.

Lenat, Douglas B., and R.V. Guha. *Building Large Knowledge-Based Systems*. Addison-Wesley, 1990.

Lewin, Roger. *Complexity, Life at the Edge of Chaos*. Macmillan, 1992.

Martin, James, and James Odell. *Object-Oriented Analysis and Design*. Prentice Hall, 1992.

Martin, James, and Steven Oxman. *Building Expert Systems*. Prentice Hall, 1988.

Martin, James. *Information Engineering (Book I, Introduction)*. Prentice Hall. 1989.

Mavrovouniotis, Michael L., ed. *Artificial Intelligence in Process Engineering*. San Diego, CA: Academic Press, 1990.

Minsky, Marvin. *The Society of Mind*. Simon and Schuster, 1986.

Newell, Allen. *Unified Theories of Cognition*. Harvard University Press, 1990.

Posner, Michael I., ed. *Foundations of Cognitive Science*. The MIT Press, 1993.

Rauch-Hindin, Wendy B. *A Guide to Commercial Artificial Intelligence*. Prentice Hall, 1988.

Rosenbloom, Paul S., and John E. Laird, et al. *The Soar Papers*. The MIT Press, 1993.

Rumbaugh, James, and Michael Blaha, et al. *Object-Oriented Modeling and Design*. Prentice Hall, 1991.

Shaw, M. J., U. Menon, et al. "Machine Learning in Knowledge-Based Process Planning Systems." *Expert Systems: Strategies and Solutions in Manufacturing Design and Planning*. Dearborn, MI, Society of Manufacturing Engineers, 1988.

Terwilliger, John P. "Process Planning for Electronic Assembly." Masters of Science in Industrial Engineering. Purdue University, 1985.

Waldrop, Mitchell M. *Complexity. The Emerging Science at the Edge of Order and Chaos*. Touchstone, 1992.

Winston, Patrick Henry. *Artificial Intelligence*. Addison-Wesley, 1984.

Zozaya-Gorostiza, Carlos, Chris Hendrickson, and Daniel R. Rehak. *Knowledge-Based Process Planning for Construction and Manufacturing*. San Diego, CA: Academic Press, 1989.

SOURCES

The following is a list of articles by the author that have been revised and reprinted in this book.

"Legacy Knowledge-based Systems," *Object Magazine* December, 1997

"Teaching Java a Thing or Two," *Object Magazine* August, 1997

"Redefining Knowledge," *PC AI* July/August, 1997

"The Joy of Remote Programming," *PC AI* May/June, 1997

"Testing the Logic," *Object Magazine* May, 1997

"Immutable Knowledge," *Object Magazine* February, 1997

"Revisiting Methodology," *Object Magazine* November, 1996

"Rethinking Artificial Intelligence," (also wrote:"Introduction to AI and Objects, OO AI Buyers Guide" (Guest Editor on the Issue) *Object Magazine* August, 1996

"Opening up to CLOS," *Object Magazine* June, 1996

"Knowledge, reuse, and change," *Object Magazine* April, 1996

"The Problem with Persistence," *Object Magazine* February, 1996

"Rediscovering Human Intelligence," *Object Magazine* Nov./Dec., 1995

"Ruling classes: The heart of knowledge-based systems," *Object Magazine* July/August, 1995

"What's the deal with Agents," *Object Magazine* May, 1995

"Learning How to Know (The Persistence of Intelligence)," *Object Magazine* February, 1995

"Learning How to Know," *Object Magazine* October, 1994

"MIS Intelligence," *Object Magazine* September, 1994

"Intelligent Information Engineering," *PC AI* July/August, 1993

"The state of AI and its O-O products," *Object Magazine* June, 1994

"Top ten reasons to use AI for client/server," *Object Magazine* May, 1994

"What Can We Learn from AI?" *Object Magazine* Feb., 1994

"Taming the AI Madness with Object Methods," *Object Magazine* Nov./Dec., 1993

"Merging Objects and Knowledge Bases," *Object Magazine* May/June, 1993

"AI and objects on the shop floor," *Object Magazine* May/June, 1993

"Objects and AI," *Object Magazine* July/August, 1992

"The Manufacturing Mind: Process Planning 102," *PC AI* July/Aug., 1991

"The Manufacturing Mind: Process Planning 101," *PC AI* May/June, 1991

"The Manufacturing Mind: Where AI Meets the Shop Floor," *PC AI* Nov./Dec., 1989

INDEX

for knowledge management,
187–189
for PC, 153
traffic routing, computer networks
for, 101
Trilogy, products and address
of, 220
Trinzic Corporation, 54, 88, 90,
213
TRUE condition, for rules, 123
Truth Maintenance System (TMS),
of Ilog Rules, 211
Turing test, of computers, 100, 101
Twain, Mark, 23, 24

U
Union Pacific Railroad, Rail Train
Scheduler of, 140
U.S. Government, use of AI
technologies by, 46, 183
University of Amsterdam, 119
University of Calgary, ICOOMS
conference at, 147
UNIX, 74, 86, 87, 123
USB, 199
user interfaces, in AI, 2

V
Valid Succeeding Work Centers,
158
Ventana Systems, 192
video games, AI and, 2
Vineyard, 118
Visual Basic, 60, 84, 180, 181, 184,
209, 215
GUI integration in, 84
Visual Recall, 118
voice recognition, 2

W
weather forecasting, agent use in, 10
The Web. *See* World Wide Web
WebLS, 205, 206

Western Digital, 65, 77, 129, 130,
131, 134, 135, 139
WHEN-NEEDED demons, of
frames, 30
widgets
of GUIs, 33, 96, 98, 125
reuse of, 96
Windows, 21, 151, 215
GUI elements in, 96
SMART use of, 138
windows, callable from
Nexpert, 43
Windows 3.1, 107
Windows 95, 67, 74, 107
Wintermute (Gibson), 25
wisdom
definition of, 113
search for, 117–118
Wisdom Systems, 147
Wizards, in Microsoft Office, 139
wizards, future use of, 68
Word, 12, 21, 55
work centers, on assembly lines,
156, 157–158, 162
workflow, 73, 82
workflow systems, information
automation by, 61
World Wide Web, 15, 74, 103, 113,
121, 187, 195
AI on, 23
ART*Enterprise support of, 207
crawlers on, 9, 23, 194
knowledge exploration by, 25

X
Xerox, 118, 154

Y
Yahoo, 121
Yourdon, Edward, 22

Z
Zeus, 6, 18